Scottish Mountaineering Club
District Guide Books

MUNRO'S TABLES

GENERAL EDITOR: A. C. D. SMALL

SCOTTISH MOUNTAINEERING CLUB

DISTRICT GUIDE BOOKS

Munro's Tables

OF THE 3000-FEET MOUNTAINS OF SCOTLAND

AND OTHER TABLES OF LESSER HEIGHTS

Edited and revised by
J. C. Donaldson and Hamish M. Brown

THE SCOTTISH MOUNTAINEERING TRUST

EDINBURGH

First published in Scotland in this edition 1981 by
THE SCOTTISH MOUNTAINEERING CLUB

Copyright © 1981 by The Scottish Mountaineering Club

First published 1891
Revised and republished 1921
Enlarged and republished 1933
New edition 1953
1953 edition revised 1969
First metric edition 1974
Reprinting history excluded
New edition 1981

ISBN 0 907521 01 0

Printed in Scotland by
Hugh K. Clarkson & Sons Ltd.,
Young Street, West Calder, West Lothian, EH55 8EQ

CONTENTS

ILLUSTRATIONS

Sir Hugh T. Munro Bart., of Lindertis

Munro's Tables

ALL THE SCOTTISH MOUNTAINS
3000 FEET IN HEIGHT AND ABOVE

Revised by the Compiler, the late
Sir HUGH T. MUNRO, BART., OF LINDERTIS
and rearranged by
Mr J. GALL INGLIS, F.R.S.E.

Edited and revised by
J. C. Donaldson and Hamish M. Brown

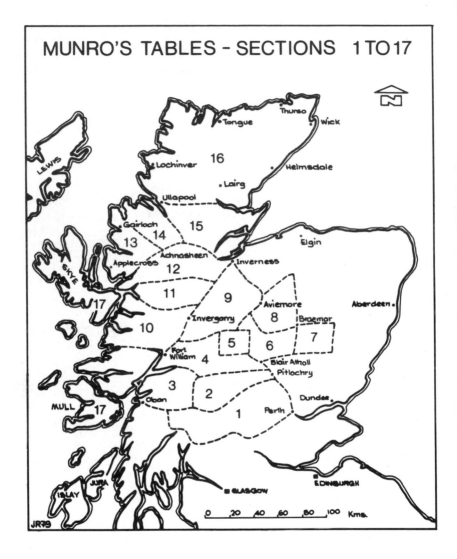

MUNRO'S TABLES - SECTIONS 1 TO 17

INTRODUCTION

THE TABLES

The original compilation of the Tables involved a tremendous amount of painstaking work at a time when little was known about the hills, and the appearance of Munro's list caused quite a stir in the then small circle of active mountaineers. Within a short time the term "Munro" was being used. The number of Munros seemed just right to make a challenge which most walkers could answer in a lifetime under the conditions of the time; many more and it would have been too onerous a task; many fewer and it would have been too easy.

Munro was working towards revised Tables when he died, so we will never know just what he would have changed. The Munros do not have a clear definition beyond the "Separate Mountain" and "Subsidiary Top" split. There is no specific re-ascent laid down as there is with Corbetts. A certain amount of "character" in a hill has affected the present revision but basically the Munros listed in this edition are the list, created by their founder, who wrote in his introduction: "the exact number cannot be determined, owing to the impossibility of deciding what should be considered distinct mountains". The years of usage have led to some changes and new maps based on more accurate surveying have produced others, and the Tables have been altered accordingly without changing the essential nature of the list.

The Editors are aware of the feelings that exist about the seemingly random or irrational nature of the selection of Mountains and Tops and they know of the arguments that have been advanced for many promotions and demotions. But if effect were to be given to all the changes proposed the Tables would no longer be "Munros". It is felt that with the coming of metrication the Tables should become an historical document and that there should be no further changes made to the list other than those made necessary when the remaining 2nd series 1:50,000 are issued. (But see the note on heights in the section "Column explanations in Table 1.) Munro acknowledged help given in his original work by Mr Colin Phillips, while footnotes in subsequent Tables and writings in the Scottish Mountaineering Club Journal through the years show the comprehensive and detailed topographical information the Club accumulated. Some of it has yet to find its way onto the O.S. maps. J. G. Inglis brought out revised Tables in 1921, reflecting many changes in the O.S. maps since 1891. Much work had also been put into this by J. R. Young and A. W. Peacock. The Corbetts and Donalds were added, both of which have been revised for this edition from the latest maps available. Changes have been made to both Tables, full details of which are given in the notes prefacing the respective groups.

The work of producing these new Tables (and the guide books to the Munros) had been held back in the hope of having the completed 2nd series 1:50,000 maps available for the areas covering Munros. However, as the few sheets remaining could be produced as late as 1990 it was felt best to proceed—and to hope that few changes would be needed then.

Hugh Thomas Munro

Munro was born in London in 1856, the son of Sir Campbell Munro of Lindertis. He was very much a Victorian figure, and dying as he did in 1919 may be said to have passed with an era. He became an original member of the Scottish Mountaineering Club when it was founded in 1889 by which time he was already a world traveller and a great walker in the hills of Scotland.

Before Sir Hugh Munro brought out his *Tables of Heights over 3000 Feet,* in the second (1891) volume of the Scottish Mountaineering Club Journal, it was generally believed that only some 30 hills were of that altitude; the authoritative Baddely's Guide, for instance, listed 31. The very first Journal had strongly hinted that the scope was far greater, possibly there were 300, not 30, "some perhaps never ascended". What could be more natural to a man like Munro than to make a tidy list of them? What could be more natural than to try to climb them all? Soon the word "Munro" appeared.

Sir Hugh was the eldest of nine children. He grew up really in two worlds, London and Scotland and as an adult he added a third, the whole world itself. When his children were old enough they went with him to Germany, Greece, Morocco, the United States, Japan, Ceylon and other lands near and far. He was a great collector as a child: fossils, eggs, butterflies and so on. Even as a young man, after a spell in South Africa, he returned with a collection of Basuto curios, antelope heads, a black boy and a monkey. He was an enthusiast with many interests all his life—a good musician and dancer for instance. He had a flow of "capital talk", no doubt like many present members of the S.M.C., though he did tend "to go on a bit" as a speaker.

His first mountain climbs were made in Germany when he was a student at Stuttgart in his late teens. He also had a business training in London. After a spell in Africa, which included serving with an irregular cavalry corps during the Basuto War, he first managed and then inherited the estate of Lindertis near Kirriemuir, which he came to regard as "home" no matter how much he wandered abroad, and his enthusiasm for the Scottish hills found its full outlet. He was the third President of the Scottish Mountaineering Club, 1894-1897. On several occasions Munro acted as King's Messenger.

Photographs of those days tend to freeze action and it was a while before shutter speeds could capture smiles. Munro was no stuffy laird but a lively and warm-hearted person; with his wide experience, talents and knowledge he enlivened any company. He would travel back from the other side of the world to attend a S.M.C. dinner or Meet. He disliked eponymous mountain names so it is a quirk of fate that his name is probably better known now than any of his contemporaries. While not a technical climber he was thoroughly capable and active, summer and winter, especially in the latter when he had more time.

Just one example to illustrate a typical Munro foray. In February 1889 he shipped to Inverie in Knoydart where the laird put him up at the lodge (he had planned to stay at the Inn). He crossed Mam Barrisdale to Skiary on Loch Hourn where he suffered the other extreme in a filthy hut which could provide little beyond oatmeal and bad whisky. He then walked up to Glen Quoich Lodge (now under Loch Quoich), lunched with the factor and had a lift to Fort Augustus. The next day he went to Drumnadrochit by steamer, through to Glen Cannich, staying overnight at Guisachan. From there he traversed Mam Sodhail and reached Shiel Inn (Loch Duich) via the Falls of Glomach. From the Inn he had a day on the Five Sisters, then crossed Mam Ratagan and Sgriol to Glenelg. The "Clansman" (steamer) took him to Glasgow and the sleeper train to London. It rather makes our car and comfort approaches seem a bit soft!

He was a great advocate and practitioner of long treks through remote areas. Often he would go alone: striding off in uniform of cape, knickerbockers (or kilt) and Balmoral bonnet, carrying a long axe and his Aneroid. Weather seldom deterred him.

There are over 80 entries in the Scottish Mountaineering Club Journal by him, many on topographical detail, for he was a whole survey in himself, and a deal more accurate than the Ordnance Survey who took another 80 years to produce reliable maps to parts of the north west. When the railways were built and motor cars invented he gladly enrolled these new fangled gadgets as an aid to exploring the hills. They were exciting days of development.

Munro never quite completed the ascent of the Munros he had listed. Carn Cloich-mhuillin above the Dee he had saved for last as it was reasonably near Lindertis and an easy ascent for a pleasant day of jollification. And then there was the Inaccessible Pinnacle, the end of many a Munroist's dreams. He was driven out from Skye by atrocious weather in 1895; in 1897 a Yachting Meet could not even anchor off Scavaig; in 1905 arrangements with Harold Raeburn (the tiger of his day) fell through. In 1906 he did the Pinnacle Ridge of Gillean, in 1908 some other Skye peaks. He was there as late as 1915 but without success.

He was past military age in 1914 but went out to work in Malta for the Red Cross and in 1918 he and two daughters organised a canteen in Tarascon in Provence. The following spring a chill developed into pneumonia and he died, aged 63.

Further information about Munro can be found in the very full obituary notice which appeared in volume 15 of the S.M.C. Journal, pages 214-219.

The Rev. A. E. Robertson was the first man to complete all the Munros (1901) and is another great figure in Scottish mountaineering. He was President of the Scottish Mountaineering Club in 1930-1932 and his climbing took him to the Alps as well. He was a fine mountaineer.

Like Munro his talents were many and the Journal is full of both his writing and his photographs; some of the latter are superb—taken with a heavy whole-plate camera as they were! Archibald Eneas Robertson had the advantage of a Rannoch parish and was often able to take three months off at a time. In two such successive holidays he gained 72 and 75 Munros respectively. As he also climbed and had other interests besides Munros, these were special sorties really. It took what he called "a desultory campaign of about 10 years" to tick them all off.

His first hill had been Goat Fell on Arran, climbed alone, aged 12 or so, when he chose to scramble the last 1000 feet to the summit. He married twice and died in 1958 aged 88.

It is hard to picture the hills before tarred roads, railways, cars—the things which we all take for granted. A.E.R. made good use of a push bike, and a pony trap or boat would help at times, but largely he walked, like Munro, often on great through trips, finding accommodation with shepherds and keepers, for speaking their Gaelic tongue and with so many common interests, he was always a welcome guest—even when he arrived with no warning. He stayed with the McCooks at Ben Alder on many occasions—and in a note in the Journal thoroughly demolished the myth of McCook's suicide. He was meticulous in every way: good gear and careful planning, accurate observation and reporting, a fascination with history, a gift for fine photography were typical of his approach. Eye and hand made him an expert carpenter.

He was chairman of the Scottish Rights of Way Society and a Fellow of the Royal Scottish Geographical Society (as was Munro) and wrote many interesting articles on "coffin" roads and such topics. The bridge over the River Elchaig on the way to the Falls of Glomach was built as a memorial to him. He had kept the Aonach Eagach for his final Munro, an expedition he made with his wife and his oldest friend, Alexander (later Lord) Moncrieff, who humorously reported A.E.R. kissing both the Meall Dearg cairn and his wife—in that order.

Both Munro and Robertson showed a thoroughly practical approach to the hills without losing anything of the romantic appeal. This is possibly a combination needed by any Munro-bagger.

A quite remarkable 22 years went by before there was a repeat. The slaughter of the First World War was no doubt partly to blame. The Rev. A. R. A. Burn in 1923 not only repeated the Munros but added the subsidiary Tops. J. A. Parker, Munroist number three, in 1929, added the "Furth of Scotland"—the resonant term for the 3000-ers of England, Wales and Ireland, which was coined by Maxwell who for long kept a list of those "quod eriat faciendum". With the uncertainty of the slump and high unemployment, it was a very different world to the leisured and assured one of Munro and the S.M.C. founding fathers, but just as an "explosion" was happening on the climbing scene, so a new enthusiasm was taking people into the hills generally. The Scottish Youth Hostels Association came into being. Hiking and biking flourished. It was glorious escapism for all classes. But despite this activity only eight people had done the Munros before World War II.

The thirties saw the new road to Glen Coe opened. Public transport was still freely available. Indeed, John Dow, No. 5, wrote in 1933 "the ascent of 277 Munros under modern road conditions is very far from being a feat". (How much more so 50 years later!) Dow pointed out that he was the first man to complete them without the help of a beard, and, it might be deduced from his delightful article in Vol. xx of the Journal that he considered a beard to be an artificial aid to climbing.

In 1949 Willie Docherty (No. 13) made the first "grand slam" of Munros, Tops and "Furth of Scotland", a surprisingly late date for this. Perhaps it is symptomatic of our present-day approach that only a dozen or so out of the 150-200 Munroists have completed everything. Doing the Munros has become an immensely popular activity, made so much easier with the weekend and holiday leisure everyone now enjoys—and the common use of the car. It used to be a life-time ambition to accomplish the Munros, now it is common place—and often done much earlier in life. Like rock-climbing, it has become, if not everyone's game, at least anyone's game.

Monroist No. 4 was J. Rooke Corbett in 1930, who of course compiled (and climbed) the list of 2500 ft. summits—the post graduate course for Munroists. Most combinations have now happened. Mrs Hirst in 1947 completed the first female round, and also a husband-wife combination. The Macdonalds in 1958 saw a father-and-son Munro effort, and in 1974 there was a Lawsons father-and-son Munros and Tops success. Anne Littlejohn made "the grand slam" in 1960. In 1964 Philip Tranter did them all again, something which several people have now managed and again a reflection on the leisure time available. They have been done by pupils of a single school, by a dog, in a single expedition; yet the appeal still lies in their being sufficiently hard and sufficiently numerous to make it a real challenge. They may be done in a youthful romp or in a lifetime of stolen moments but the reward is the same. They are not open to competition so retain their amateur status and varied approach. The editors' only plea is to the gentler walker: do not leave the Cuillin till last! We know too many fine old friends who "have done them all, except Skye".

There are probably as many Munroists living in Sheffield and Manchester as there are in all Scotland; fortunately Scotland has the hills and England the cities from which with true dedication the English set out on the Munro trail; any long weekend or holiday sees an invasion from the south. By the time you have done all the Munros you know Scotland as few others can and you know it in all its climatic variations. (If you have driven 800 miles to climb a few hills, you climb a few hills.) Dreaming of it, planning it, packing for it, this is all part of the game. The pubs and chip shops en route, the A9 roadworks, huts, bothies and camps all become part of the game. Others may slack or funk foul weather, the Munroist goes forth to war regardless, and now and then is blessed beyond belief. The whole rich experience of the hills is his. There are rock-climbers who just climb rock. They have their reward, but the Munroist is driven, willy-nilly to a wider experience in every way. He is seldom just a Munroist.

Some people have suggested the 3000 foot altitude should be changed to the tidy 1000 metre mark. This suggestion meets with little approval. Munro's Tables would not be Munro's Tables if so emasculated. Too easy a task would remove the essential challenge. As their pursuit (and even their definition) is irrational, the historical and traditional aspects demand we keep the *status quo*. It is interesting to see that the new *metric* Bartholomew's map specifically marks Munros. (In contrast the Ordnance Survey still refuse to name some of them or give them a height though they have been with us for over 80 years.) No, a list of 3282 foot peaks would not be the Munros!

The list of people who had done the Munros which appeared in the last edition of the Tables has been continued but it is known that not every one who does all the Munros reports the fact so that the list cannot be taken as complete. The list is maintained by the Editor of the Scottish Mountaineering Club Journal but it was Eric Maxwell of the Grampian Club, Dundee, who began the catalogue. In successive issues of the Grampian Club Journal he listed "all who, to the best of the author's knowledge have climbed every Munro and, also, which of them have climbed other mountains and tops in Munro's and/or Maxwell's Tables". Maxwell did the grand slam and was the first to do the Munros and tops twice. There are notes on Munroists, usually highly entertaining and including information supplied by Maxwell, in all issues of the Scottish Mountaineering Club Journal from 1961 onwards. Many other articles on Munros and Maxwells are scattered throughout the Journals from 1890 to the present day.

Most of this biographical note is based on the similar chapter from *Hamish's Mountain Walk* (Gollancz 1978) and various stories about Munro are scattered in that account of doing all the Munros. Richard Gilbert's small book *Memorable Munros* (Advertiser Office, York) has culled various accounts as well. Campbell Steven's *The Story of Scotland's Hills* (Hale 1975) is also full of interesting history.

Editors' Notes

Munros

Throughout the life of the Tables there has been discussion on the seemingly random or irrational nature of elevation to the Munro peerage. Munro left no definition, indeed had none, so what constitutes a Munro is bound to be subjective. Strong cases have been made for many promotions and demotions but the editors have made only a few changes to remove the worst anomalies without basically altering the Tables as Munro envisaged them.

Tops

An effort has been made to rationalise these many elevations over the 3000 foot level. Many have been removed as they present an insufficient rise or definition to really merit any title. A few have been added due to changes on maps. Several double-topped summits have had their lower member enrolled as a "Top"—probably a more valid and certainly clearer use of the word "Top" than its regular employment for minor bumps which can be a long way from the summit proper.

The alterations to Munros and Tops are listed at the end of the prefatory notes.

Lay-out

This has been simplified by removing some columns and also clarified by introducing collective names for groups within the Sections which have been renumbered for more convenient use with the guide books. A few groups have changed their section. (For instance, the Aonach Eagach is placed with Glen Coe, not the Mamores.) The numbering of the Sections are from South to North, 1 to 9 covering the area south of the Great Glen, 10 to 6 that to the North, with 17 covering Skye and Mull as before.

Column Explanations in Table I

Column 1. Name The O.S. 2nd series 1:50,000 names/spellings are used wherever possible as this is the standard walkers' map. These names/spellings are not always correct, or there may be variations or local differences. Larger scale maps, previous editions of the Tables, or other sources have been used where the present O.S. map has not given a name. In a few cases names have been changed to conform with alterations in the O.S. maps.

Column 2. Height The O.S. 2nd series 1:50,000 heights are followed, where given. Larger scale maps or other sources have been used where heights are missing. In some cases it will be found that heights quoted in the Tables differ from those shown on 2nd series 1:50,000 maps the O.S. having already revised them. Historic heights in feet are not given as they may not be accurate due to the various changes made as the result of new surveys and the changeover to the metric system. Conversion back from metres to feet will in many cases produce differing heights. 3000 feet = 914.4m, which excludes Beinn Dearg (Torridon), height 2998 feet. c denotes a contour.

Columns 3 and 4. Munros/Tops. These are listed numerically, the separate mountains styled Munros in column 3 and the hills without separate status, referred to as "Tops", in column 4.

Columns 5 and 6. 5 gives the number of the 2nd series 1:50,000 map(s) on which the Munros appear and 6 the numbers of the Bartholomew maps, 1:100,000 National series.

Column 6. Map References. An explanation of their use appears on all O.S. 1:50,000 maps and this is further elaborated in the Munro Guidebooks.

Maps. The following are the O.S. maps (1:50,000) required to cover the Munros:
9 15 16 19 20 25 32 33 34 35 36 40 41 42 43 44 48 50 51 52 56 57.
In the case of Bartholomew's the numbers are: 44 47 48 50 51 52 54 55 58 59 60.
Also recommended are:
S.M.C. The Black Cuillin, Island of Skye (James Renny) 1:15,000.
O.S. Outdoor Leisure Map: The Cuillin and Torridon Hills 1:25,000.
O.S. Outdoor Leisure Map: High Tops of the Cairngorms 1:25,000.

THE GEOGRAPHICAL SECTIONS

South of the Great Glen

1. The country south of a line from Oban, Dalmally, Strath Fillan, Loch Tay and on to the A9.
2. The area bounded by the West Highland railway, Loch Rannoch, the A9, Loch Tay, Glen Dochart, Strathfillan to Bridge of Orchy.
3. The area bounded by Loch Linnhe, Loch Leven, the Blackwater Reservoir, the West Highland railway, Bridge of Orchy, Tyndrum and Oban.
4. The area bounded by upper Loch Linnhe, Glen Spean, Loch Ericht, Blackwater Reservoir, Loch Leven.
5. The hills on either side of the A9 at the Drumochter Pass.
6. The area bounded by Glen Tromie, Glen Geldie, Braemar, the A90 to Perth, the A9 through Blair Atholl and the Gaick Pass.
7. The country east of the A93 Braemar-Perth road and south of the River Dee from Braemar to Aberdeen.
8. The country east and north of the Glen Feshie, Glen Geldie, Braemar-Aberdeen line.
9. The area bounded by the Great Glen, the A9 from Inverness to Newtonmore and the A86 from Newtonmore to Spean Bridge.

North of the Great Glen

10. The mainland south of Glen Shiel and Glen Moriston and West of the Great Glen.
11. The Area north of Glen Shiel and Glen Moriston, and south of Loch Mullardoch, bounded in the west by the coast, and in the east by the Great Glen.
12. The area south of the Kyle of Lochalsh—Beauly railway and north of a line from Kyle of Lochalsh—Loch Mullardoch to Cannich, with Cannich—Beauly forming the eastern boundary.
13. The area west of the Kyle of Lochalsh-Achnasheen railway and south of a line from Achnasheen to Poolewe.
14. The area north of the road from Garve through Achnasheen to Poolewe and south of the road from Garve to Loch Broom.
15. The country between the Inverness-Garve-Ullapool road and a line from Ullapool to Lairg.
16. The country north of the Lochinver-Lairg road.
17. The Islands of Mull and Skye.

Details of changes to Munros and Tops

The 1974 edition of *Munro's Tables* listed 279 Munros and 541 Tops. The corresponding numbers in this edition are 276 and 517.

Munros

Number listed in 1974	279
Add—already reported—section 12 (new numbering)	
Sgurr nan Ceannaichean	1
after revision by editors	
New Section 4 Mamores—Sgor an Iubhair	
10 Loch Nevis—Garbh Chioch Mhor	
13 Liathach—Mullach an Rathain	
14 An Teallach—Sgurr Fiona	4
	284

284

Deduct—already reported—Section 1 (old numbering)
  Beinn an Lochain (height 901m)   1

after revision by editors

Old Section 8	Carn Cloich-mhuillin		
	Meal Dubhag		
	Carn Ban Mor		
	Geal Charn		
	A' Choinnich		
9	Monadh Liath:—		
	Carn Ban		
	Carn Balloch	7	8

276

Tops

Number listed in 1974	541
Add new Tops	19
	560
Less Tops deleted	43
	517

Names of new Tops

New Section   1. Ben Lui—North West Top.
             4. Sgor an Iubhair—Stob a' Choire Mhail.
             7. Creag Leacach—South West Top.
                White Mounth—Eagle's Rock.
             8. Carn a' Chlamain—North Top.
                Bynack More—Bynack Beg.
           10. Meall Buidhe—South East Top.
                Luinne Bheinn—East Top.
                The Saddle:
                  Trig Point
                  East Top
                Sgurr na Sgine—North West Top.
           12. An Riabachan—North East Top (not to be confused with the North East Top in the 1974 edition which was and still is the main summit).
                An Riabachan—West Top.
                An Riabachan—South West Top.
                Sgurr nan Ceannaichean.
           14. Mullach Coire Mhic Fhearchair:—
                  East Top
                  Sgurr Dubh.
                Slioch North Top.
                A' Chailleach—Toman Coinich.

Names of Tops deleted

Old Section   1. Beinn an Lochain.

            3. Carn Mairg Range:—
                Meall Luaidhe.
                Meall Buidhe—South East Top.
                Beinn Heasgarnich—Stob an Fhir Bhoga.

            4. Clach Leathad Range—Mam Coire Easain.

            5. Carn Mor Dearg—Carn Beag Dearg.
                Aonach Mor—Stob Coire an Fhir Dhuibh.
                Stob Choire Claurigh—North Top.
                Mullach Coire an Iubhair—Sron Garbh.

            6. Carn Liath—A' Bhuidheanach.
                Carn Ban—Snechdach Slinnean.

            8. Sgurr nan Ceathreamhnan—Creag nan Clach Geala.
                Mullach Fraoch-choire—North East Top.
                Mam Sodhail:—
                    Stob Coire Coulavie
                    Ciste Dubh.
                Carn Eighe—Creag na h-Eighe.

            9. Sgurr na Lapaich:—
                Rudha ma Spreidhe.
                Creag a' Chaorainn.
                Braigh a' Choire Bhig.
                Creag Toll a' Choin.

           10. Beinn Eighe—Creag Dhubh.

           12. Ben Wyvis—Fiaclach.

           14. Ben Avon:—
                South West Top.
                Stob Bac an Fhurain.
                Mullach Lochan nan Gobhar.
                Stuc Gharbh Mhor.
                Stob Dubh an Eas Bhig.
                Beinn a' Bhuird—A' Chioch.
                Derry Cairngorm—Little Cairngorm.
                Ben Macdui—Stob Coire Sputan Dearg.
                Cairngorm:—
                    Fiacaill Coire an t-Sneachda.
                    Fiacaill a' Choire Chais.
                    Sron a' Cha-no.
                    Creag an Leth-choin—North Top.
                    Fiacaill na Leth-choin.
                Braeriach—Stob Coire an Lochain.
                Mullach Clach a' Bhlair—Diollaid Coire Eindart.

           15. A' Bhuidheanach Bheag—Meall a' Chaorainn.
                An Sgarsoch—Druim Sgarsoch.
                Beinn Dearg—Beinn Gharbh.
                Carn nan Sac.

           16. Cairn Bannoch—Creag Leachdach.
                Lochnagar—Little Pap.

Finally, the editors acknowledge their indebtedness to Sir Hugh Munro and to all those who subsequently assisted with revisions of the Tables for the help this has been in preparing this new Edition. Thanks are due to those who supplied illustrations and diagrams, to D. J. Fraser for permission to include *The Lost Leader,* and especially to the staff of the National Library of Scotland for much assistance given most willingly over many days in the Map Room. Appreciation is also expressed to those who wrote to the editors about the inclusion or exclusion of a number of hills in the three sections of the Tables, all the comments being of value.

SECTION 1

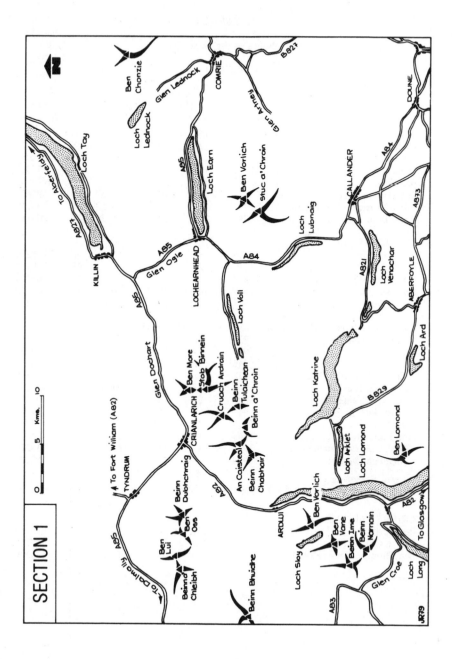

TABLE 1

South of the Great Glen

SECTION 1

NAME	Height	No. in order of Altitude Mtn.	No. in order of Altitude Top	Map Sht. Nos. O.S.	Map Sht. Nos. Bart.	Map Reference
BEN LOMOND and THE ARROCHAR ALPS						
Ben Lomond	974	179	304	56	44/48	367029
Beinn Narnain	926†	255	468	56	48	272067
Beinn Ime	1011	115	194	56	48	255085
Ben Vane	915	274	514	56	48	278098
Ben Vorlich	943	225	404	56/50	48	295125
Ben Vorlich—North Top . . .	931	—	444	56/50	48	294130
Beinn Bhuidhe	948	212	385	56/50	48	204187
TYNDRUM GROUP						
Beinn a'Chleibh	916	273	511	50	48	251256
Ben Lui (Beinn Laoigh)	1130	27	44	50	48	266263
Ben Lui—North West Top . .	1127	—	48	50	48	265264
Ben Oss	1029	100	167	50	48	287253
Beinn Dubhchraig	978	171	290	50	48	308255
CRIANLARICH, BALQUIDDER and GLEN FALLOCH						
Beinn Chabhair	933	242	439	50/56	48	367180
An Caisteal	995	144	243	50/56	48	379193
Beinn a' Chroin	946*	216	393	50/56	48	394186
Beinn a' Chroin—West Top.	938*	—	423	50/56	48	386185
Beinn Tulaichean	946	218	395	51/56	48	416196
Cruach Ardrain	1046	83	141	51	48	409211
Stob Garbh	959	—	352	51	48	411221
Ben More	1174	15	25	51	48	432244
Stob Binnein	1165	17	28	51	48	434226
Stob Coire an Lochain	1068	—	114	51	48	438220
Meall na Dige	966	—	328	51	48	452226

†*927m on 1:10,000 map.*
**Heights shown on O.S. sheets 50/56 differ. The correct heights for Beinn a' Chroin and the West Top are as given above.*

CRIEFF and LOCH EARN						
Ben Vorlich	985	161	269	57	48	629189
Stuc a' Chroin	975	176	300	57	48	617175
Ben Chonzie (Ben-y-Hone) . . .	931	245	443	51	48	773309

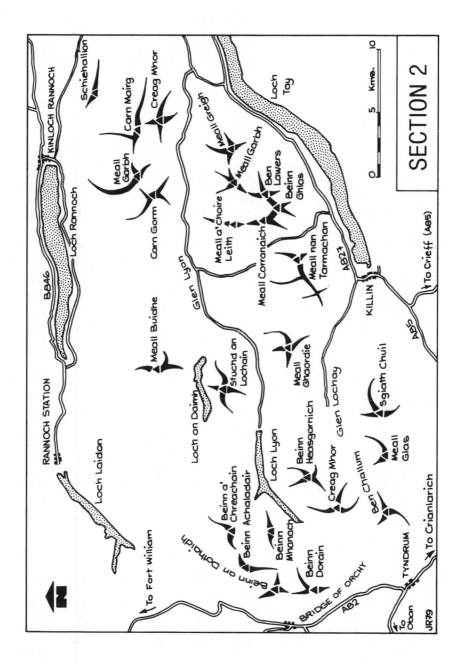

SECTION 2

SECTION 2

NAME	Height	No. in order of Altitude Mtn.	Top	Map Sht. Nos. O.S.	Bart.	Map Reference
RANNOCH—GLEN LYON						
Schiehallion..................	1083	57	94	51	48	714548
Carn Mairg.................	1042	87	150	51	48	684513
Meall Liath...............	1012	—	193	51	48	692511
Meall a' Bharr	1004	—	213	51	48	668516
Creag Mhor	981	167	280	51	48	695496
Meall Garbh.................	963	186	333	51	48	651515
An Sgor	924	—	477	51	48	641509
Carn Gorm.................	1029	99	166	51	48	635501
Stuchd an Lochain	960	193	348	51	48	483449
Sron Chona Chorein.......	918	—	502	51	48	494446
Meall Buidhe	931	244	442	51	48	498499
THE LAWERS GROUP						
Ben Lawers.................	1214	9	14	51	48	636414
Creag an Fhithich	1047	—	139	51	48	635423
An Stuc...................	1118	—	56	51	48	639430
Meall Garbh.................	1118	35	55	51	48	644437
Meall Greigh	1001	134	222	51	48	674438
Bheinn Ghlas	1103	45	75	51	48	626404
Meall Corranaich	1069	65	110	51	48	616410
Meall a' Choire Leith	926	257	470	51	48	612439
Meall nan Tarmachan........	1043	86	148	51	48	585390
Meall Garbh...............	1026	—	172	51	48	578383
Beinn nan Eachan	1000c	—	226	51	48	569384
Creag na Caillich..........	916	—	512	51	48	563377
MAMLORN						
Meall Ghaordie	1039	89	153	51	48	514397
Beinn Heasgarnich	1076	61	102	51	48	413383
Creag Mhor	1032	96	162	51	48	391361
Stob nan Clach	958	—	356	50	48	387352
Ben Challum	1025	103	173	50	48	387322
Ben Challum—South Top ..	997	—	239	50	48	386316
Meall Glas	960	192	347	50	48	431322
Beinn Cheathaich	937	—	429	51	48	444327
Sgiath Chuil................	935	237	433	51	48	463318
Meall a' Churain	918	—	500	51	48	463326
BRIDGE OF ORCHY HILLS						
Beinn Dorain	1074	62	103	51	48	326378
Beinn an Dothaidh	1002	130	216	50	48	332408
Beinn Achaladair............	1039	90	154	50	48	344432
Beinn Achaladair— South Top	1002	—	219	50	48	342421
Beinn a' Chreachain	1081	59	98	50	48	373441
Meall Bhuidhe	977	—	294	50	48	359439
Beinn Mhanach	954	205	369	50	48	373412
Beinn a' Chuirn	924	—	475	50	48	360411

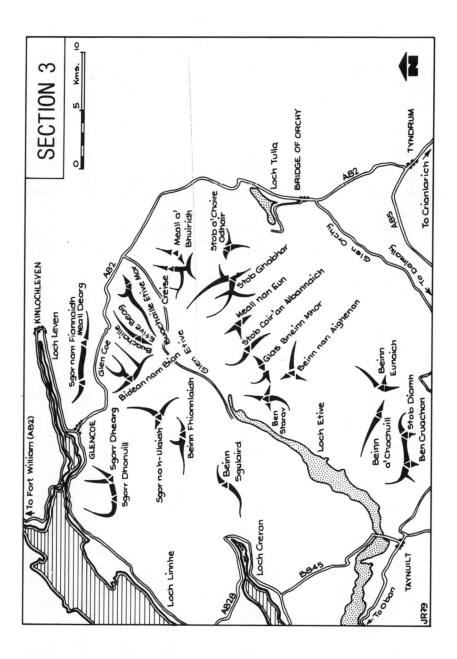

SECTION 3

SECTION 3

NAME	Height	No. in order of Altitude		Map Sht. Nos.		Map Reference
		Mtn.	Top	O.S.	Bart.	
CRUACHAN GROUP						
Ben Cruachan	1126	31	49	50	47	069304
Stob Dearg (Taynuilt Peak).	1101	—	77	50	47	062307
Meall Cunail	918	—	504	50	47	069295
Drochaid Glas	1009	—	201	50	47	083306
Stob Diamh	998	141	236	50	47	095308
Stob Garbh...............	980	—	289	50	47	095302
Sron an Isean	966	—	327	50	47	099311
Beinn a' Chochuill...........	980	168	284	50	47	110328
Beinn Eunaich	989	152	258	50	48/47	136328
ETIVE HILLS						
Beinn nan Aighenan	957	201	360	50	47/48	149405
Ben Starav	1078	60	101	50	47/48	126427
Meall Cruidh	930	—	450	50	47/48	129416
Stob Coire Dheirg	1068	—	115	50	47/48	131426
Glas Bheinn Mhor...........	997	142	238	50	47/48	153429
Stob Coir' an Albannaich.....	1044	85	146	50	47/48	169442
Meall nan Eun	928	250	457	50	47/48	192449
THE CORRIE BA RANGE						
Stob Gabhar.................	1087	54	90	50	48	230455
Stob a' Bruaich Leith	939	—	419	50	47/48	208459
Sron a' Ghearrain	991c	—	253	50	48	221457
Sron nam Giubhas.........	974	—	307	50	48	231462
Aonach Eagach	991c	—	252	50	48	236454
Stob a' Choire Odhair........	943	224	403	50	48	258461
Creise	1100	48	79	41	48	238507
Clach Leathad	1098	—	81	41	48	240493
Stob a' Ghlais Choire	996	—	241	41	48	240516
Meall a' Bhuiridh	1108	43	68	41	48	251503
GLENCOE						
Buachaille Etive Mor-Stob						
Dearg	1022	106	176	41	48	223543
Stob na Doire.............	1011	—	195	41	48	207533
Stob Coire Altruim	939	—	420	41	48	197531
Stob na Broige............	955	—	366	41	48	191526
Buachaille Etive Beag-Stob						
Dubh....................	958	196	353	41	47/48	179535
Stob Coire Raineach	925	—	472	41	47/48	191548
Bidean nam Bian	1150*	23	36	41	47/48	143542
Stob Coire nam Beith	1107	—	70	41	47/48	139546
Stob Coire nan Lochan.....	1115	—	60	41	47/48	148459
Stob Coire Sgreamhach	1072	—	106	41	47/48	155536
Beinn Fhada...............	952	—	377	41	47/48	159541
Beinn Fhada—						
North East Top..........	931	—	445	41	47/48	164543

Table I. *Arranged according to Districts* 17

SECTION 3 *(continued)*

NAME	Height	No. in order of Altitude Mtn.	Top	Map Sht. Nos. O.S.	Bart.	Map Reference
AONACH EAGACH						
Sgor nam Fiannaidh	967	182	323	41	47/50	141583
Stob Coire Leith	940	—	414	41	47/50	149585
Meall Dearg	953	208	374	41	47/50	161584
Am Bodach	943	—	405	41	47/50	168580
APPIN						
Sgor na h'Ulaidh	994	146	245	41	47	111518
Stob an Fhuarain..........	968	—	322	41	47	118523
Beinn Fhionnlaidh...........	959	195	351	50	47	095498
Beinn Sgulaird	937	233	427	50	47	053461
Beinn a' Bheithir:						
Sgorr Dhonuill..............	1001	132	220	41	47	040555
Sgorr Dhearg	1024	104	174	41	47	056558
Sgorr Bhan...............	947	—	391	41	47	063560

*Bidean nam Bian. The highest point is not shown on the O.S. 1:50,000 map.

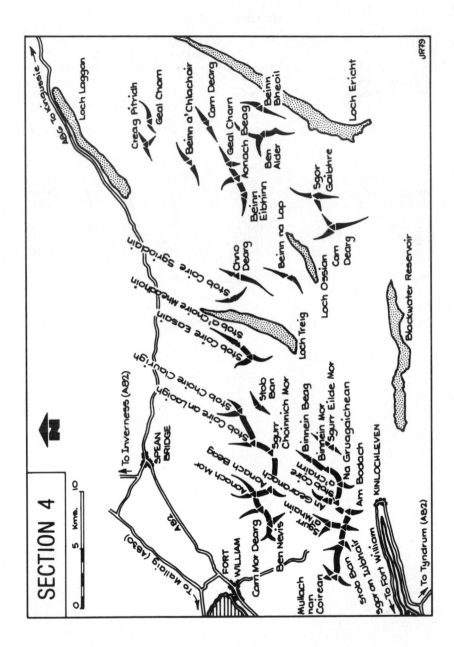

SECTION 4

N

0   5   Kms.   10

To Kingussie ➤

A86

Loch Laggan

Creag Pitridh

Geal Charn

Beinn a'Chlachair

Carn Dearg

Geal Charn

Beinn Bheoil

Aonach Beag

Ben Alder

Beinn Eibhinn

Sgor Gaibhre

Beinn na Lap

Loch Ossian

Carn Dearg

Loch Ericht

Chno Dearg

Stob Coire Sgriodain

Stob a'Choire Mheadhoin

Stob Coire Easain

Loch Treig

Blackwater Reservoir

To Inverness (A82)

SPEAN BRIDGE

Stob Choire Claurigh

Stob Ban

Stob Coire an Laoigh

Sgurr Choinnich Mor

Binnein Beag

Binnein Mor

Sgurr Eilde Mor

Na Gruagaichean

Am Bodach

To Mallaig (A830)

Carn Mor Dearg

Ben Nevis

Aonach Mor

Aonach Beag

Sgurr a'Mhaim

An Gearanach

Stob Coire a'Chairn

KINLOCHLEVEN

FORT WILLIAM

Mullach nan Coirean

Stob Ban

Sgor an Iubhair

To Fort William

To Tyndrum (A82)

JR79

Table I. Arranged according to Districts 19

SECTION 4

NAME	Height	No. in order of Altitude Mtn.	No. in order of Altitude Top	Map Sht. Nos. O.S.	Map Sht. Nos. Bart.	Map Reference
THE MAMORES						
Sgurr Eilde Mor.............	1008	120	202	41	48/50/51	231658
Binnein Beag	940	228	412	41	48/50/51	222677
Binnein Mor.................	1128	30	47	41	48/50/51	212663
Binnein Mor—South Top...	1059	—	120	41	48/50/51	211657
Sgurr Eilde Beag	956	—	363	41	48/50/51	219653
Na Gruagaichean............	1055	71	122	41	48/50/51	203652
Na Gruagaichean— North West Top.........	1036	—	157	41	48/50/51	201654
An Gearanach	982	162	275	41	48/50/51	187670
An Garbhanach...........	975	—	303	41	48/50/51	188665
Stob Coire a' Chairn........	981	165	278	41	48/50/51	185661
Am Bodach	1032	95	161	41	48/50/51	176651
Sgor an Iubhair	1001	133	221	41	48/50/51	165655
Stob a' Choire Mhail.......	970c	—	316	41	48/50/51	163659
Sgurr a' Mhaim	1099	49	80	41	48/50/51	165667
Stob Ban....................	999	138	232	41	48/50/51	148654
Mullach nan Coirean	939	231	418	41	50	122662
Mullach nan Coirean— South East Top	917	—	510	41	50	131655
BEN NEVIS and THE AONACHS						
Ben Nevis..................	1344	1	1	41	50/51	166713
Carn Dearg— South West Top.........	1020	—	181	41	50/51	155701
Carn Dearg— North West Top.........	1221	—	11	41	50/51	159719
Carn Mor Dearg	1223	7	10	41	50/51	177722
Carn Dearg Meadhonach ...	1180	—	21	41	50/51	176727
Aonach Mor.................	1219c	8	12	41	50/51	193730
Stob an Cul Choire	1097	—	83	41	50/51	203732
Tom na Sroine.............	918	—	499	41	50/51	208745
Aonach Beag	1236	6	9	41	50/51	196715
Stob Coire Bhealaich	1097c	—	82	41	50/51	202709
Sgurr a' Bhuic	965	—	331	41	50/51	204702
GREY CORRIES						
Sgurr Choinnich Mor	1095	50	84	41	50/51	227714
Sgurr Choinnich Beag......	966	—	326	41	50/51	220710
Stob Coire an Laoigh	1115	37	59	41	50/51	240725
Stob Coire Easain	1080	—	99	41	50/51	234727
Caisteal..................	1104	—	74	41	50/51	246729
Beinn na Socaich	1007	—	206	41	50/51	236734
Stob Coire Cath na Sine	1080	—	100	41	50/51	252731
Stob Choire Claurigh	1177	14	22	41	50/51	262739
Stob a' Choire Leith	1105c	—	73	41	50/51	256736
Stob Coire Gaibhre........	930c	—	447	41	50/51	260757
Stob Coire na Ceannain	1121	—	50	41	50/51	268746

SECTION 4 (continued)

NAME	Height	No. in order of Altitude Mtn.	Top	Map Sht. Nos. O.S.	Bart.	Map Reference
Stob Ban....................	977	173	293	41	50/51	266724
Stob Coire Easain	1116	36	58	41	51	308730
Stob a' Choire Mheadhoin....	1106	44	71	41	51	316736
LOCH TREIG and LOCH OSSIAN						
Stob Coire Sgriodain.........	976	174	296	41	51	356744
Stob Coire Sgriodain— South Top	960	—	349	41	51	359739
Chno Dearg	1047	81	138	41	51	377741
Meall Garbh..............	977	—	295	41	51	372727
Beinn na Lap	937	232	426	41	51	376696
Carn Dearg.................	941	226	410	42	51	418661
Sgor Gaibhre	955	203	364	42	51	444674
Sgor Choinnich	929	—	454	42	51	443683
LOCH ERICHT to LOCH LAGGAN						
Beinn Eibhinn	1100	47	78	42	51	448733
Mullach Coire nan Nead....	921	—	485	42	51	431734
Meall Ghlas Choire	922c	—	480	42	51	438729
Aonach Beag	1114	38	61	42	51	458742
Geal-Charn	1132	25	41	42	51	470746
Sgor Iutharn..............	1014c	—	189	42	51	490743
Carn Dearg.................	1034	94	160	42	51	504764
Diollaid a' Chairn	922	—	481	42	51	488758
Beinn a' Chlachair...........	1088	53	89	42	51	471781
Creag Pitridh	924	260	474	42	51	488814
Geal Charn.................	1049	78	134	42	51	504812
Ben Alder	1148	24	38	42	51	496718
Bheinn Bheoil	1019	110	183	42	51	517717
Sron Coire na h'Iolaire.....	955	—	367	42	51	513704

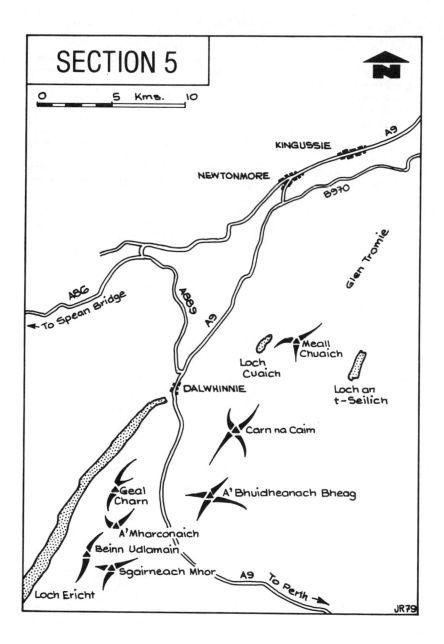

SECTION 5

0   5 Kms. 10

N

A9
KINGUSSIE
NEWTONMORE
B970
Glen Tromie
A86
To Spean Bridge →
A889
A9
Loch
Cuaich
Meall
Chuaich
Loch an
t-Seilich
DALWHINNIE
Carn na Caim
Geal
Charn
A'Bhuidheanach Bheag
A'Mharconaich
Beinn Udlamain
Sgairneach Mhor
A9 To Perth →
Loch Ericht

JR79

SECTION 5

NAME	Height	No. in order of Altitude		Map Sht. Nos.		Map Reference
		Mtn.	*Top*	*O.S.*	*Bart.*	
THE DRUMOCHTER HILLS						
Sgairneach Mhor............	991	151	254	42	51	599731
Beinn Udlamain.............	1010	119	199	42	51	579739
A' Mharconaich	975	178	302	42	51	604763
Geal Charn.................	917	272	507	42	51	598783
Meall Chuaich	951	209	379	42	51	716879
Carn na Caim...............	941	227	411	42	51	677822
A' Bhuidheanach Bheag......	936	234	430	42	51	661776
Glas Mheall Mor	928	—	462	42	51	681769

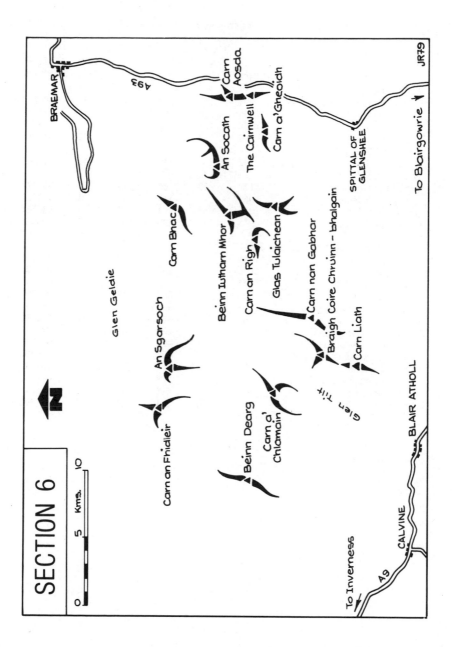

SECTION 6

0   5   10
Kms.

N

To Inverness

A9

CALVINE

BLAIR ATHOLL

To Blairgowrie

SPITTAL OF
GLENSHEE

Glen Tilt

Glen Geldie

BRAEMAR

A93

Carn an Fhidleir

An Sgarsoch

Carn Bhac

Beinn Dearg

Carn a'
Chlamain

Beinn Iutharn Mhor

Carn an Righ

Glas Tulaichean

Carn nan Gabhar

Braigh Coire Chruinn – bhalgain

Carn Liath

An Socach

The Cairnwell

Carn a'Gheoidh

Carn
Aosda

JR79

SECTION 6

NAME	Height	No. in order of Altitude Mtn.	Top	Map Sht. Nos. O.S.	Bart.	Map Reference
THE TARF and TILT HILLS						
Carn an Fhidleir or Carn Ealar	994	145	244	43	51	905842
An Sgarsoch................	1006	124	208	43	51	933836
Beinn Dearg................	1008	121	203	43	51	853778
Carn a' Chlamain	963	187	334	43	51	916758
Carn a' Chlamain— North Top	952	—	378	43	51	914761
Beinn a' Ghlo:						
Carn nan Gabhar............	1129	29	46	43	51	971733
Airgiod Bheinn	1061	—	118	43	51	962720
Braigh Coire Chruinn-bhalgain	1070	63	107	43	51	946724
Carn Liath	975	175	299	43	51	936698
WEST of the CAIRNWELL PASS						
Glas Tulaichean.............	1051	77	130	43	51/52	051760
Carn an Righ	1029	98	165	43	51/52	028772
Beinn Iutharn Mhor	1045	84	143	43	51/52	045792
Mam nan Carn............	986	—	267	43	51/52	049799
Beinn Iutharn Bheag.......	953	—	375	43	51/52	065791
Carn Bhac	946	217	394	43	51/52	051832
Carn Bhac—South West Top	920	—	489	43	51/52	041827
An Socach—West Summit	944	222	400	43	51/52	079799
An Socach—East Summit ..	938	—	421	43	51/52	099806
Carn a' Gheoidh	975	177	301	43	51/52	107767
Carn Bhinnein	917	—	508	43	51/52	091762
The Cairnwell	933	241	438	43	51/52	135773
Carn Aosda	917	270	505	43	51/52	134792

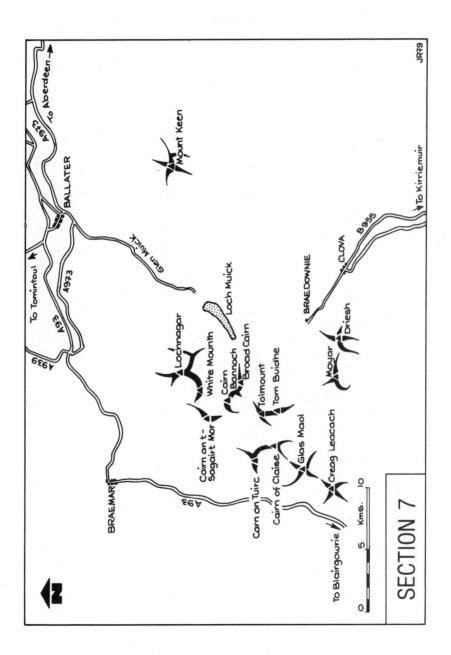

SECTION 7

SECTION 7

NAME	Height	No. in order of Altitude Mtn.	Top	Map Sht. Nos. O.S.	Bart.	Map Reference
GLAS MAOL HILLS						
Glas Maol..................	1068	67	112	43	52	166765
Meall Odhar..............	922	—	482	43	51/52	156773
Little Glas Maol...........	973	—	311	43	51/52	175758
Creag Leacach..............	987	157	264	43	51/52	155745
Creag Leacach—						
South West Top.........	943	—	406	43	51/52	149741
Cairn of Claise..............	1064	68	116	43	52	185789
Druim Mor...............	961	—	340	43	52	190771
Carn an Tuirc...............	1019	112	185	43	52	174804
GLEN DOLL HILLS						
Tom Buidhe.................	957	199	358	43	52	214788
Tolmount...................	958	198	355	44	52	210800
Crow Craigies	920	—	492	44	52	222798
Cairn Bannoch..............	1012	114	192	44	52	223825
Fafernie	1000	—	228	44	52	215823
Cairn of Gowal	983	—	273	44	52	227817
Craig of Gowal	991	—	256	44	52	226821
Broad Cairn.................	998	139	234	44	52	240815
Creag an Dubh-loch	983	—	272	44	52	233823
Mayar.....................	928	248	455	44	52	241738
Driesh.....................	947	213	388	44	52	271736
LOCHNAGAR and WHITE MOUNTH						
Lochnagar-Cac Carn Beag....	1155	19	31	44	52	244861
Lochnagar-Cac Carn Mor ..	1150	—	37	44	52	245857
Meall Coire na Saobhaidhe .	974	—	309	44	52	243873
Cuidhe Crom..............	1083	—	95	44	52	260849
Meikle Pap...............	980	—	288	44	52	260861
White Mounth:—						
Carn a' Choire Bhoidheach ...	1118	33	53	44	52	226845
Creag a' Ghlas-uillt........	1068	—	113	44	52	242842
Top of Eagle's Rock	1051	—	132	44	52	237838
Carn an t-Sagairt Beag	1044	—	147	44	52	216848
Carn an t-Sagairt Mor........	1047	80	137	44	52	208843
Mount Keen................	939	229	416	44	52	409869

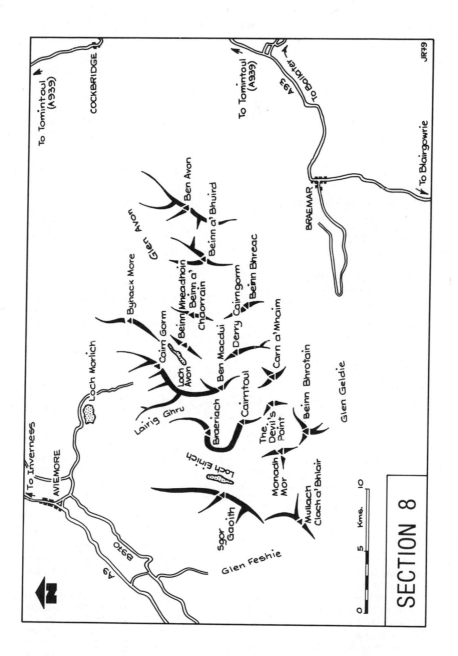

SECTION 8

SECTION 8

NAME	Height	No. in order of Altitude Mtn.	Top	Map Sht. Nos. O.S.	Bart.	Map Reference
GLEN FESHIE HILLS						
Mullach Clach a' Bhlair	1019	111	184	43	51	883927
Meall Dubhag	998	—	237	43	51	881956
Carn Ban Mor	1052	—	129	43	51	893972
Sgor Gaoith	1118	34	54	43/36	51	903989
Sgoran Dubh Mor	1111	—	64	36	51	905002
Meall Buidhe	976	—	297	36	51	891001
Geal Charn................	920	—	490	36	51	884014
WESTERN CAIRNGORMS						
Braeriach	1296	3	3	36	51	953999
Sron na Lairige	1184	—	17	36	51	964006
Carn na Criche............	1265	—	6	36	51	939983
Tom Dubh	918	—	503	36	51	921952
Cairn Toul	1291	4	5	36	51	963972
Stob Coire an t-Saighder ...	1213	—	15	36	51	962963
Sgor an Lochain Uaine	1258	—	7	36	51	954976
The Devil's Point............	1004	127	212	36/43	51	976951
Monadh Mor	1113	39	62	43	51	938942
Beinn Bhrotain	1157	18	30	43	51	954923
Carn Cloich-mhuilinn......	942	—	409	43	51	968907
MACDUI—CAIRNGORM						
Carn a' Mhaim	1037	92	156	36	51/52	994952
Ben Macdui	1309	2	2	36	51/52	989989
Ben Macdui—North Top ...	1295	—	4	36	51/52	991995
Sron Riach	1110	—	67	36	51/52	999978
Cairn Etchachan	1120	—	52	36	51/52	003009
Cairn Gorm	1245c	5	8	36	51/52	005040
Creag an Leth-choin (Lurcher's Crag)	1053	—	127	36	51/52	968033
Cairn Lochan.............	1215	—	13	36	51/52	985025
Stob Coire an t-Sneachda ...	1176	—	24	36	51/52	996029
Cnap Coire na Spreidhe	1151	—	34	36	51/52	013049
LAIRIG an LAOIGH HILLS						
Bynack More	1090	52	87	36	51/52	042063
Bynack Beg	964	—	332	36	51/52	035068
A' Choinneach............	1017	—	186	36	51/52	032048
Beinn Mheadoin	1182	12	19	36	51/52	024016
Beinn Mheadoin— South West Top.........	1163	—	29	36	51/52	018011
Stob Coire Etchachan	1082	—	97	36	51/52	024005
Stacan Dubha	1013	—	191	36	51/52	012014
Derry Cairngorm............	1155	20	32	36	51/52	017980
Sgurr an Lochan Uaine.....	983	—	274	36	51/52	025991
Creagan a' Choire Etchachan	1108	—	69	36	51/52	012996

Table I.   Arranged according to Districts   29

SECTION 8 *(continued)*

NAME	Height	No. in order of Altitude Mtn.	Top	Map Sht. Nos. O.S.	Bart.	Map Reference
Beinn Bhreac	931	243	441	36	51/52	058970
Beinn Bhreac—West Top...	927	—	466	36	51/52	052972
Beinn a' Chaorainn..........	1082	58	96	36	51/52	045013
Beinn a' Chaorainn Bheag ..	1015	—	187	36	51/52	058018

EASTERN CAIRNGORMS
Ben Avon:

NAME	Height	No. in order of Altitude Mtn.	Top	Map Sht. Nos. O.S.	Bart.	Map Reference
Leabaidh an Daimh Bhuidhe..	1171	16	27	36	51/52	132019
East Meur Gorm Craig	935	—	434	36	51/52	159042
West Meur Gorm Craig	1021	—	178	36	51/52	154035
Carn Eas.................	1089	—	88	36	51/52	122992
Creag an Dail Mhor	972	—	313	36	51/52	132982
Beinn a' Bhuird—North Top..	1196	10	16	36	51/52	092005
South Top	1177	—	23	36	51/52	090978
Cnap a' Cleirich...........	1172	—	26	36	51/52	108009
Stob an t-Sluichd..........	1106	—	72	36	51/52	112027

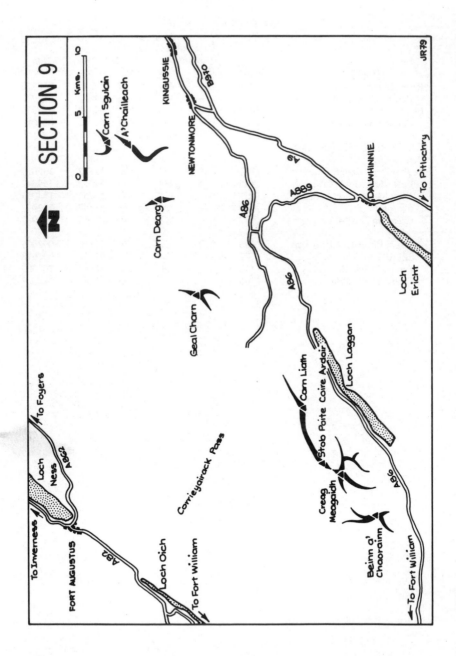

SECTION 9

Table I. *Arranged according to Districts* 31

SECTION 9

NAME	Height	No. in order of Altitude Mtn.	Top	Map Sht. Nos. O.S.	Bart.	Map Reference
LOCH LAGGAN HILLS						
Beinn a' Chaorainn..........	1052	76	128	34	51	386851
South Top	1050	—	133	34	51	386845
North Top	1045	—	144	34	51	384857
Creag Meagaidh	1130	26	43	34	51	418875
An Cearcallach	993	—	248	34	51	422854
Meall Coire Choille-Rais ...	1027	—	171	34	51	433862
Puist Coire Ardair.........	1070	—	108	34	51	436873
Sron a' Choire*	1001	—	224	34	51	448878
Stob Poite Coire Ardair	1053	75	126	34	51	429888
East Top................	1051	—	131	34	51	437892
Sron Coire a' Chriochairean	991	—	255	34	51	447899
Carn Liath	1006	123	207	34	51	472903
Meall an-t-Snaim..........	969	—	318	34	51	459905
Stob Coire Dhuibh	916**	—	513	34	51	496917
THE MONADH LIATH						
Geal Charn..........	926	256	469	35	51	561988
Carn Dearg...............	945	220	398	35	51	635024
South East Top	920c	—	486	35	51	637018
Carn Ban	942	—	407	35	51	632031
Carn Balloch	920	—	491	35	51	643045
Carn Sgulain	920	263	487	35	51	684059
A' Chailleach..............	930	247	449	35	51	681041

*O.S. Sheet 34 gives this as "Ghoire".
**O.S. only shows a contour height of 910 but the highest point is 916.

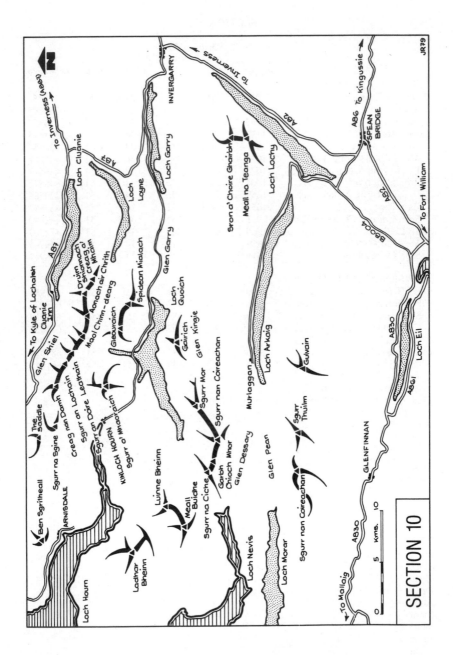

SECTION 10

Table I. Arranged according to Districts 33

North of the Great Glen

SECTION 10

NAME	Height	No. in order of Altitude Mtn.	Top	Map Sht. Nos. O.S.	Bart.	Map Reference
LOCH LOCHY HILLS						
Meall na Teanga	917	271	506	34	50	220924
Sron a' Choire Ghairbh	935	236	432	34	50	222945
GULVAIN and GLEN PEAN						
Gaor Bheinn (or Gulvain).....	987	156	263	41	50	002876
South Top	961	—	339	40	50	997864
Sgurr Thuilm	963	188	335	40	50	939879
Sgurr nan Coireachan........	956	202	361	40	50	903880
CICHE—KINGE						
Sgurr na Ciche..............	1040	88	151	33/40	50	902966
Garbh Chioch Mhor	1013	113	190	33/40	50	909961
Garbh Chioch Bheag.......	968	—	320	33/40	50	918959
Sgurr nan Coireachan........	953	207	373	33/40	50	933958
Sgurr Mor..................	1003	128	214	33/40	50	965980
Gairich	919	265	493	33	50	025995
KNOYDART and SGRITHEALL						
Meall Buidhe	946	215	392	33/40	50	849989
South East Top	930	—	451	33/40	50	853987
Luinne Bheinn	939	230	417	33/40	50	868008
East Top..................	937	—	428	33/40	50	872007
Ladhar Bheinn..............	1020	108	180	33/40	50	824040
Stob a' Choire Odhair......	960c	—	346	33/40	50	830043
Ben Sgritheall...............	974	180	305	33/40	50	836126
North West Top...........	928	—	460	33/40	50	835131
LOCH QUOICH						
Sgurr a' Mhaoraich..........	1027	101	169	33	50	984065
Sgurr a' Mhaoraich Beag ...	948	—	386	33	50	977067
Gleouraich	1035	93	159	33	50	039054
Craig Coire na Fiar Bhealaich	1006	—	209	33	50	047051
Spidean Mialach	996	143	240	33	50	066043
SOUTH GLEN SHIEL						
Creag a' Mhaim..............	947	214	389	33	50	088078
Druim Shionnach	987	155	262	33	50	074085
Aonach Air Chrith	1021	107	177	33	50	051083
Maol Chinn-dearg...........	981	166	279	33	50	032088
Sgurr an Doire Leathain......	1010	116	196	33	50	015099
Sgurr an Lochain............	1004	126	211	33	50	005104
Creag Nan Damh............	918	268	497	33	50	983112

SECTION 10 *(continued)*

NAME	Height	Mtn.	Top	O.S.	Bart.	Map Reference
THE SADDLE GROUP						
The Saddle	1010*	118	198	33	50	936131
Trig Point................	1010	—	200	33	50	934131
West Top	968c	—	319	33	50	928128
Spidean Dhomhuill Bhric...	940	—	415	33	50	922129
Sgur Leac nan Each........	919	—	494	33	50	918133
East Top.................	958	—	357	33	50	938130
Sgurr na Forcan...........	960c	—	345	33	50	941131
Sgurr na Sgine	945	221	399	33	50	946113
North West Top...........	944	—	402	33	50	944115

*Observation on the ground gives the impression that the main summit of The Saddle is slightly higher than the Trig Point.

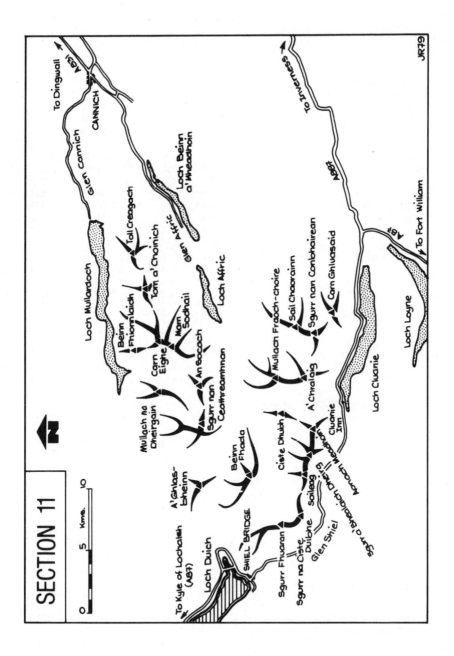

SECTION 11

SECTION 11

NAME	Height	No. in order of Altitude Mtn.	Top	Map Sht. Nos. O.S.	Bart.	Map Reference
NORTH GLEN SHIEL						
THE FIVE SISTERS to CISTE DHUBH						
Sgurr Fhuaran	1068	66	111	33	54/50	978167
Sgurr nan Saighead	929	—	453	33	54/50	975178
Sgurr na Carnach	1002	—	218	33	54/50	977159
Sgurr na Ciste Duibhe........	1027	102	170	33	54/50	984149
Sgurr nan Spainteach	990c	—	257	33	54/50	992150
Saileag	959	194	350	33	54/50	018148
Sgurr a' Bhealaich Dheirg	1038	91	155	33	54/50	035143
Aonach Meadhoin...........	1003	129	215	33	54/50	049137
Sgurr an Fhuarail	988	—	260	33	54/50	054139
Ciste Dhubh................	982	163	276	33	54/50	062166
A' CHRALAIG—CONBHAIREAN GROUP						
Mullach Fraoch-choire.......	1102	46	76	33	54/50	095171
A' Chralaig	1120	32	51	33	54/50	094148
Stob Coire na Cralaig	1008	—	204	33	54/50	091163
A' Chioch.................	948	—	387	34	54/50	108153
Sail Chaorainn..............	1002	131	217	34	54/50	133154
Carn na Coire Mheadhoin ..	1001	—	223	34	54/50	134159
Tigh Mor na Seilge	929	—	452	34	54/50	141166
Sgurr nan Conbhairean	1110	42	66	34	54/50	129139
Drochaid an Tuill Easaich ..	1000	—	229	34	54/50	121134
Creag a' Chaorainn........	999	—	233	34	54/50	137131
Carn Ghluasaid	957	200	359	34	54	146125
GLEANN LICHD—GLEN AFFRIC						
A' Ghlas-bheinn	918	269	498	25/33	54	008231
Beinn Fhada (Ben Attow).....	1032	97	163	25/33	54	018192
Meall an Fhuarain Mhoir ...	956	—	362	25/33	54	000196
Sgurr a' Dubh Doire	963	—	337	25/33	54	035185
GLEN AFFRIC						
Sgurr nan Ceathreamhnan	1151	21	33	25/33	54	057228
West Top*	1143	—	40	25/33	54	053228
Stob Coire nan Dearcag* ...	940	—	413	25/33	54	071225
Stuc Bheag	1074	—	105	25/33	54	053237
Stuc Mor*................	1043	—	149	25/33	54	054243
Mullach na Dheiragain	982	164	277	25/33	54	091259
Mullach Sithidh*..........	973	—	312	25/33	54	082264
Carn na Con Dhu*	968	—	321	25/33	54	073242
An Socach	920	264	488	25/33	54	088230
Mam Sodhail	1180	13	20	25	54	120253
Creag Coire nan Each......	1056	—	121	25	54	113234
An Tudair.................	1074	—	104	25	55	127239
Mullach Cadha Rainich	993	—	249	25	55	139246
Sgurr na Lapaich..........	1036	—	158	25	55	154243

Table I. *Arranged according to Districts* 37

SECTION 11 *(continued)*

NAME	Height	No. in order of Altitude Mtn.	Top	Map Sht. Nos. O.S.	Bart.	Map Reference
Carn Eighe................	1183	11	18	25	54	123262
Stob Coire Lochan	917	—	509	25	54	119272
Stob a' Choire Dhomhain ..	1148	—	39	25	54	133265
Sron Garbh	1132	—	42	25	55	145264
Beinn Fhionnlaidh...........	1005	125	210	25	55	115282
Tom a' Choinich	1111	40	63	25	55	163273
Tom a' Choinich Beag	1029	—	168	25	55	157273
An Leth-chreag	1044c	—	145	25	55	153269
Toll Creagach	1054	73	124	25	55	194283
Toll Creagach—West Top ..	952	—	376	25	55	177275

The names of the tops marked with an asterisk are not shown on the 1:50,000 map.

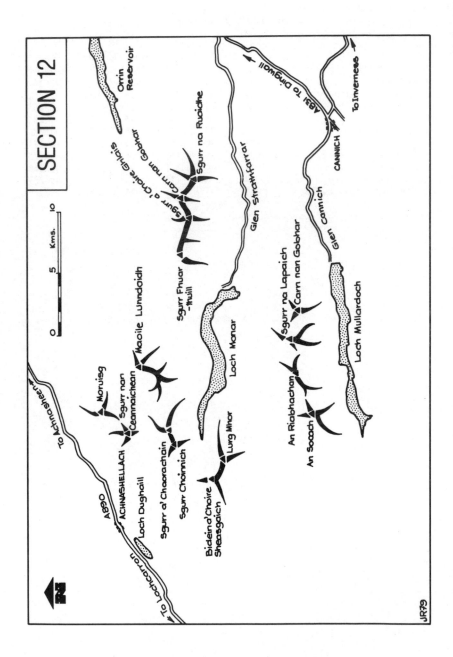

SECTION 12

Table I. Arranged according to Districts 39

SECTION 12

NAME	Height	No. in order of Altitude Mtn.	Top	Map Sht. Nos. O.S.	Bart.	Map Reference
SGURR NA LAPAICH GROUP						
Carn nan Gobhar	992	150	251	25	55	182344
Creag Dhubh	946	—	396	25	55	200351
Sgurr na Lapaich	1150	22	35	25	55	161351
Sgurr nan Clachan Geala ...	1095	—	85	25	55	162342
An Riabhachan	1129	28	45	25	55	134345
North East Top	1117c	—	57	25	55	139348
South West Top...........	1086	—	91	25	55	123338
West Top	1040	—	152	25	55	117336
An Socach	1069	64	109	25	55	100332
THE STRATHFARRAR HILLS						
Sgurr na Ruaidhe............	993	148	247	25	55	289425
Carn nan Gobhar	992	149	250	25	55	273439
Sgurr a' Choire Ghlais	1083	56	93	25	55	259430
Sgurr Fhuar-thuill	1049	79	135	25	55	236437
Creag Ghorm a' Bhealaich..	1030	—	164	25	55	244435
Sgurr na Fearstaig	1015	—	188	25	55	228437
EAST of ACHNASHELLACH						
Moruisg	928	252	459	25	54	101499
Sgurr nan Ceannaichean......	915	275	515	25	54	087480
Maoile Lunndaidh...........	1007	122	205	25	54	135458
Carn nam Fiaclan	996	—	242	25	54	123454
Sgurr a' Chaorachain	1053	74	125	25	54	087447
Bidean an Eoin Dearg......	1046	—	142	25	54	103443
Sgurr Choinnich	999	136	230	25	54	076446
Bidein a' Choire Sheasgaich...	945	219	397	25	54	049412
Lurg Mhor	986	158	265	25	54	065404
Meall Mor	974	—	308	25	54	072405

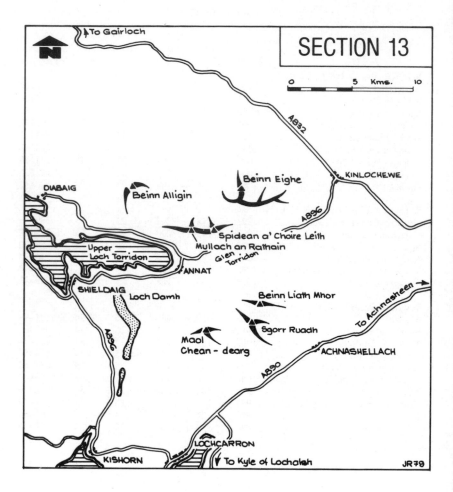

SECTION 13

To Gairloch

N

0   5 Kms. 10

A832

KINLOCHEWE

DIABAIG

Beinn Eighe

Beinn Alligin

A896

Spidean a' Choire Leith
Mullach an Rathain

Upper
Loch Torridon

Glen
Torridon

ANNAT

SHIELDAIG

Loch Damh

Beinn Liath Mhor

To Achnasheen

A896

Sgorr Ruadh

Maol
Chean - dearg

ACHNASHELLACH

A890

LOCHCARRON

KISHORN

To Kyle of Lochalsh

JR79

Table I.   Arranged according to Districts   41

SECTION 13

NAME	Height	No. in order of Altitude Mtn.	Top	Map Sht. Nos. O.S.	Bart.	Map Reference
STRATH CARRON—GLEN TORRIDON						
Maol Chean-dearg..........	933	240	437	25	54	924498
Sgorr Ruadh................	960c	191	343	25	54	959504
Beinn Liath Mhor	925	258	471	25	54	964519
THE TORRIDONS						
Beinn Alligin—Sgurr Mhor ...	985	160	268	19	54	866613
Tom na Gruagaich.........	922	—	484	19	54	859601
Liathach—						
Spidean a' Choire Leith	1054	72	123	25	54	929579
Mullach an Rathain..........	1023	105	175	25	54	912577
Northern Pinnacles........	953c	—	372	25	54	914579
Am Fasarinen	927	—	465	25	54	924575
Stob a' Coire Liath Mhor...	983c	—	271	25	54	933581
Beinn Eighe-Ruadh-Stac-Mor .	1010	117	197	19	54	951611
Sail Mhor	981	—	281	19	54	938605
A' Choinneach Mhor	975c	—	298	19	54	944600
Spidean Coire nan Clach ...	972	—	314	25	54	965597
Sgurr Ban................	971	—	315	25	54	974600
Sgurr an Fhir Duibhe	963	—	336	25	54	982600

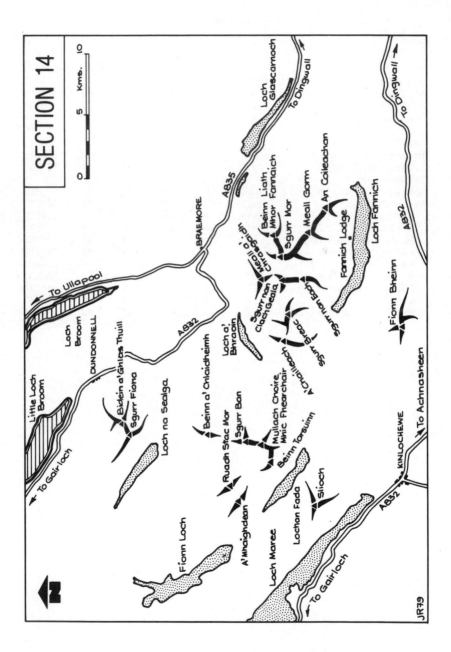

SECTION 14

0   5   Kms.   10

To Ullapool

Little Loch Broom

Loch Broom

DUNDONNELL

Bidein a'Ghlas Thuill
Sgurr Fiona

To Gairloch

Loch na Sealga

Fionn Loch

A'Mhaighdean

Ruadh Stac Mor

Beinn a' Chlaidheimh

Sgurr Ban

Loch a' Bhraoin

Mullach Coire
Mhic Fhearchair

Beinn Tarsuinn

A'Crualleach

Loch Maree

Lochan Fada

Slioch

To Gairloch

KINLOCHEWE

A832

To Achnasheen

A832

BRAEMORE

A835

Meall a'
Chrasgaidh

Sgurr nan
Clach Geala

Sgurr Breac

Sgurr nan Each

Beinn Liath
Mhor Fannaich

Sgurr Mor

Meall Gorm

An Coileachan

Fannich Lodge

Loch Fannich

Fionn Bheinn

A832

To Dingwall

Loch Glascarnoch

To Dingwall

JR79

Table I. Arranged according to Districts 43

SECTION 14

NAME	Height	No. in order of Altitude Mtn.	Top	Map Sht. Nos. O.S.	Bart.	Map Reference
SLIOCH—AN TEALLACH GROUP						
Slioch—Trig Point	980	169	285	19	54	005688
North Top	980	—	287	19	54	004691
Sgurr an Tuill Bhain	933	—	440	19	54	018689
Ruadh Stac Mor	918	267	496	19	58	018756
A' Mhaighdean	960c	190	342	19	54	007748
Beinn Tarsuinn	930c	246	446	19	54	039727
Mullach Coire Mhic Fhearchair	1019	109	182	19	58	052735
East Top.................	981	—	283	19	58	056734
Sgurr Dubh	918	—	501	19	58	061729
Sgurr Ban.................	989	153	259	19	58	055745
Beinn a' Chlaidheimh	914	276	517	19	58	061775
An Teallach—						
Bidein a' Ghlas Thuill........	1062	69	117	19	58	069843
Glas Mheall Mor	981	—	282	19	58	076854
Glas Mheall Liath	950c	—	380	19	58	077841
Sgurr Fiona	1059	70	119	19	58	064837
Sgurr Creag an Eich	1000c	—	225	19	58	055838
Lord Berkeley's Seat	1047c	—	136	19	58	064834
Corrag Bhuidhe...........	1020c	—	179	19	58	065833
Corrag Bhuidhe Buttress ...	937c	—	424	19	58	066831
Stob Cadha Gobhlach......	950c	—	381	19	58	068825
Sail Liath	954	—	371	19	58	071824
THE FANNAICHS						
A' Chailleach..............	999	137	231	19	54	136714
Toman Coinich	937c	—	425	19	54	148714
Sgurr Breac	1000	135	227	20	54/55	158711
Meall a' Chrasgaidh	934	238	435	20	55	184733
Sgurr nan Clach Geala	1093	51	86	20	55	184715
Sgurr nan Each	923	262	479	20	55	184697
Sgurr Mor.................	1110	41	65	20	55	203718
Carn na Criche...........	961	—	341	20	55	196725
Meall nam Peithirean	974	—	306	20	55	207708
Beinn Liath Mhor Fannaich...	954	204	368	20	55	219724
Meall Gorm	949	210	383	20	55	221696
South East Top	922	—	483	20	55	232692
An Coileachan..............	923	261	478	20	55	241680
Fionn Bheinn..............	933	239	436	20	55	147621

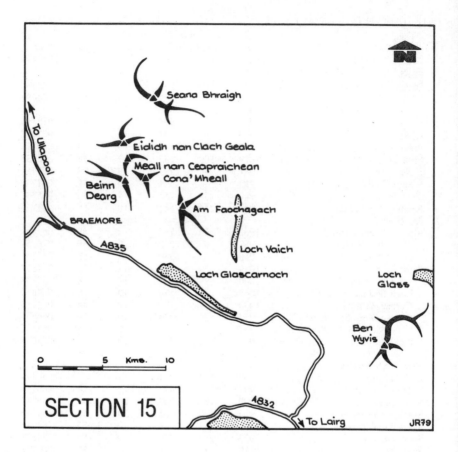

Seana Bhraigh

Eididh nan Clach Geala

Meall nan Ceapraichean
Cona' Mheall

Beinn
Dearg

Am Faochagach

Loch Vaich

BRAEMORE

To Ullapool

A835

Loch Glascarnoch

Loch
Glass

Ben
Wyvis

0   5   Kms.   10

A832

To Lairg

SECTION 15

JR79

Table I. Arranged according to Districts 45

SECTION 15

NAME	Height	No. in order of Altitude Mtn.	Top	Map Sht. Nos. O.S.	Bart.	Map Reference
BEN WYVIS and the BEINN DEARG GROUP						
Ben Wyvis—						
Glas Leathad Mor	1046	82	140	20	59	463684
An Cabar	950	—	382	20	59	450665
Tom a' Choinnich	955	—	365	20	59	463700
Glas Leathad Beag	928	—	461	20	59	492706
Am Faochagach.............	954	206	370	20	58	303793
Cona' Mheall	980	170	286	20	58	274816
Beinn Dearg	1084	55	92	20	58	259812
Meall nan Ceapraichean	977	172	292	20	58	257825
Ceann Garbh	967	—	324	20	58	259831
Eididh nan Clach Geala	928	249	456	20	58	257842
Seana Braigh	927	254	464	20	58	281878

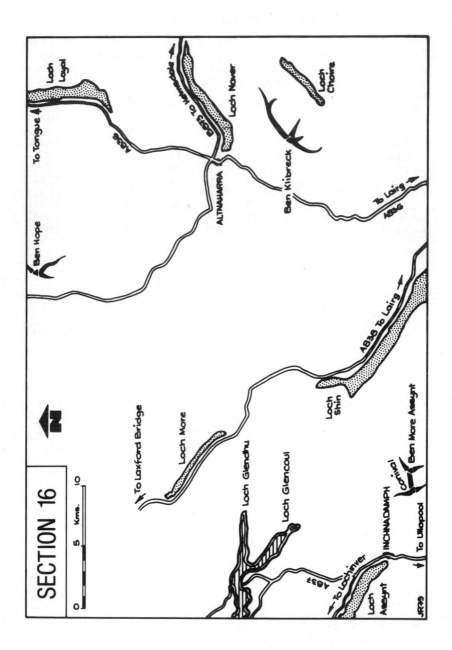

SECTION 16

0　5　10
Kms.

N

To Tongue
Loch Loyal
To Helmsdale
B873
Loch Naver
Loch Choire
A836
Ben Hope
ALTNAHARRA
Ben Klibreck
To Lairg
A836
To Laxford Bridge
Loch More
A836 To Lairg
Loch Shin
Loch Glendhu
Loch Glencoul
INCHNADAMPH
Conival
Ben More Assynt
To Lochinver
A837
To Ullapool
Loch Assynt
JRR9

Table I. *Arranged according to Districts* 47

SECTION 16

NAME	Height	No. in order of Altitude		Map Sht. Nos.		Map Reference
		Mtn.	*Top*	*O.S.*	*Bart.*	
ASSYNT						
Ben More Assynt............	998	140	235	15	58	318201
South Top	960c	—	344	15	58	324193
Conival...................	987	154	261	15	58	303199
HOPE and KLIBRECK						
Ben Hope.................	927	253	463	9	60	477501
Ben Klibreck	961	189	338	16	60	585299

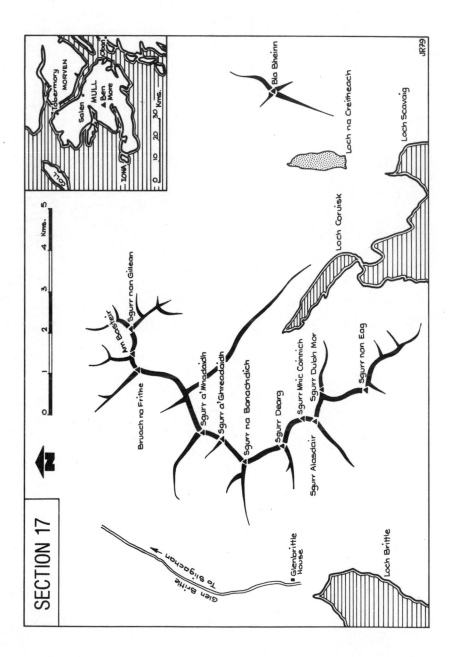

SECTION 17

Sgurr nan Gillean
Am Basteir
Bruach na Frithe
Sgurr a'Mhadaidh
Sgurr a'Ghreadaidh
Sgurr na Banachdich
Sgurr Dearg
Sgurr Mhic Coinnich
Sgurr Dubh Mor
Sgurr Alasdair
Sgurr nan Eag

Glen Brittle
To Sligachan
Glenbrittle House
Loch Brittle

Loch Coruisk
Bla Bheinn
Loch na Creitheach
Loch Scavaig

0 1 2 3 4 Kms. 5

COLL
IONA
TOBERMORY
MORVEN
MULL
Salen
Ben More
Oban
0 10 20 30 Kms.

JR79

Table I. Arranged according to Districts 49

SECTION 17

The Islands

NAME	Height	No. in order of Altitude Mtn.	Top	Map Sht. Nos. O.S.	Bart.	Map Reference
MULL						
Ben More	966	183	325	48	47	526331
SKYE						
THE CUILLIN						
SLIGACHAN HILLS						
Sgurr nan Gillean	965	185	330	32	54	472253
Am Basteir	935	235	431	32	54	465253
Bhasteir Tooth............	914c	—	516	32	54	464252
Bruach na Frithe	958	197	354	32	54	461252
Sgurr a' Fionn Choire......	930c	—	448	32	54	463252
THE CENTRAL CUILLIN						
Sgurr a' Mhadaidh	918	266	495	32	54	446235
Sgurr a' Ghreadaidh	973	181	310	32	54	445232
South Top	969	—	317	32	54	445229
GLEN BRITTLE HILLS						
Sgurr na Banachdich.........	965	184	329	32	54	440225
Central Top	942	—	408	32	54	442222
Sgurr Thormaid...........	927	—	468	32	54	441226
Sgurr Dearg—						
Inaccessible Pinnacle	986	159	266	32	54	444215
Sgurr Dearg—Cairn	978	—	291	32	54	443216
Sgurr Mhic Coinnich.........	948	211	384	32	54	450210
Sgurr Alasdair	993	147	246	32	54	449208
Sgurr Thearlaich	984	—	270	32	54	451208
Sgurr Sgumain............	947	—	390	32	54	448206
THE SOUTHERN CUILLIN						
Sgurr Dubh Mor	944	223	401	32	54	457205
Sgurr Dubh na Da Bheinn ..	938	—	422	32	54	455204
Sgurr nan Eag	924	259	473	32	54	457195
Bla Bheinn (Blaven)	928	251	458	32	54	530217
South West Top...........	924	—	476	32	54	528215

TABLE II

THE 3000-FEET TOPS ARRANGED IN ORDER OF ALTITUDE

No. in order of Alt. Mtn.	Top	Height	Name	Sect. in Table I
1	1	1344	Ben Nevis	4
2	2	1309	Ben Macdui	8
3	3	1296	Braeriach	8
–	4	1295	Ben Macdui—North Top	8
4	5	1291	Cairn Toul	8
–	6	1265	Carn na Criche.	8
–	7	1258	Sgor an Lochain Uaine	8
5	8	1245c	Cairn Gorm	8
6	9	1236	Aonach Beag	4
7	10	1223	Carn Mor Dearg	4
–	11	1221	Carn Dearg—North West Top.	4
8	12	1219c	Aonach Mor.	4
–	13	1215	Cairn Lochan.	8
9	14	1214	Ben Lawers.	2
–	15	1213	Stob Coire an t-Saighdeir	8
10	16	1196	Beinn a' Bhuird—North Top	8
–	17	1184	Sron na Lairige	8
11	18	1183	Carn Eighe.	11
12	19	1182	Beinn Mheadoin	8
13	20	1180	Mam Sodhail	11
–	21	1180	Carn Dearg Meadhonach	4
14	22	1177	Stob Choire Claurigh	4
–	23	1177	Beinn a' Bhuird—South Top	8
–	24	1176	Stob Coire an t-Sneachda	8
15	25	1174	Ben More	1
–	26	1172	Cnap a' Cleirich.	8
16	27	1171	Ben Avon—Leabaidh an Daimh Bhuidhe	8
17	28	1165	Stob Binnein	1
–	29	1163	Beinn Mheadoin—South West Top . . .	8
18	30	1157	Beinn Bhrotain	8
19	31	1155	Lochnagar—Cac Carn Beag	7
20	32	1155	Derry Cairngorm.	8
21	33	1151	Sgurr nan Ceathreamhnan	11
–	34	1151	Cnap Coire na Spreidhe	8
22	35	1150	Sgurr na Lapaich.	12
23	36	1150	Bidean nam Bian	3
–	37	1150	Lochnagar—Cac Carn Mor	7
24	38	1148	Ben Alder	4
–	39	1148	Stob a' Choire Dhomhain	11
–	40	1143	Sgurr nan Ceathreamhnan—West Top.	11
25	41	1132	Geal-Charn	4
–	42	1132	Sron Garbh	11
26	43	1130	Creag Meagaidh	9
27	44	1130	Ben Lui.	1
28	45	1129	An Riabhachan	12

Ben Cruachan—The Summit with Ben Dearg beyond

D. J. Bennet

Ben Lawers—Looking towards Meall Garbh and An Stuc from Meall Corranaich

Lochnagar

Coire an Lochain. A spring thaw has produced Scotland's only glacier

Buchaille Etive Mor from Black Rock

Aonach Beag—the eastern cliffs

H. M. Brown

On the Grey Corries ridge, looking towards Stob Coire an Laoigh

D. J. Bennet

Sgurr na Ciche and Garbh Chioch Mor from the west   *D. J. Bennet*

The Saddle from Glen Shiel

H. M. Brown

H. M. Brown

Ben Sgritheall from the east

Looking north-east from Beinn Bhan to the Achnashellach hills

D. J. Bennet

Ben Alligin over Loch Torridon

H. M. Brown

Letterewe: looking over Fionn Loch to Ruadh Stac Mor (centre) and A' Mhaighdean (right)

D. J. Bennet

Ben Loyal, the northernmost Corbett from Ben Hope, the most northerly Munro

H. M. Brown

Arran: A' Chir (left), Caisteal Abhail and Cir Mhor (right), from Beinn a' Chliabhain

D. J. Bennet

Askival, one of the Rhum Corbetts and the highest peak on the island

Skye: Sgurr Mhic Choinnich—Sgurr Alasdair

Bla Bheinn

D. J. Bennet

Table II.   Arranged in Order of Altitude   51

No. in order of Alt. Mtn.	Top	Height	Name	Sect. in Table I
29	46	1129	Beinn a' Ghlo—Carn nan Gabhar.......	6
30	47	1128	Binnein Mor........................	4
–	48	1127	Ben Lui—North West Top...........	1
31	49	1126	Ben Cruachan	3
–	50	1121	Stob Coire na Ceannain	4
32	51	1120	A' Chralaig	11
–	52	1120	Cairn Etchachan	8
33	53	1118	White Mounth—Carn a' Choire Bhoidheach	7
34	54	1118	Sgor Gaoith	8
35	55	1118	Meall Garbh........................	2
–	56	1118	An Stuc............................	2
–	57	1117c	An Riabhachan—North East Top.....	12
36	58	1116	Stob Coire Easain	4
37	59	1115	Stob Coire an Laoigh	4
–	60	1115	Stob Coire nan Lochan..............	3
38	61	1114	Aonach Beag (Alder District).........	4
39	62	1113	Monadh Mor	8
40	63	1111	Tom a' Choinich	11
–	64	1111	Sgoran Dubh Mor	8
41	65	1110	Sgurr Mor..........................	14
42	66	1110	Sgurr nan Conbhairean	11
–	67	1110	Sron Riach	8
43	68	1108	Meall a' Bhuiridh	3
–	69	1108	Creagan a' Choire Etchachan	8
–	70	1107	Stob Coire nam Beith	3
44	71	1106	Stob a' Choire Mheadhoin...........	4
–	72	1106	Stob an t'Sluichd..................	8
–	73	1105c	Stob a' Choire Leith	4
–	74	1104	Caisteal............................	4
45	75	1103	Bheinn Ghlas	2
46	76	1102	Mullach Fraoch-choire	11
–	77	1101	Stob Dearg (Taynuilt Peak)	3
47	78	1100	Beinn Eibhinn	4
48	79	1100	Creise	3
49	80	1099	Sgurr a' Mhaim	4
–	81	1098	Clach Leathad	3
–	82	1097c	Stob Coire Bhealaich	4
–	83	1097	Stob an Cul Choire	4
50	84	1095	Sgurr Choinnich Mor	4
–	85	1095	Sgurr nan Clachan Geala	12
51	86	1093	Sgurr nan Clach Geala	14
52	87	1090	Bynack More	8
–	88	1089	Carn Eas...........................	8
53	89	1088	Beinn a' Chlachair...................	4
54	90	1087	Stob Ghabhar	3
–	91	1086	An Riabhachan—South West Top	12
55	92	1084	Beinn Dearg........................	15
56	93	1083	Sgurr a' Choire Ghlais	12
57	94	1083	Schiehallion	2
–	95	1083	Cuidhe Crom.......................	7

No. in order of Alt. Mtn.	Top	Height	Name	Sect. in Table I
58	96	1082	Beinn a' Chaorainn..................	8
–	97	1082	Stob Coire Etchachan................	8
59	98	1081	Beinn a' Chreachain	2
–	99	1080	Stob Coire Easain	4
–	100	1080	Stob Coire Cath na Sine	4
60	101	1078	Ben Starav	3
61	102	1076	Beinn Heasgarnich	2
62	103	1074	Beinn Dorain	2
–	104	1074	An Tudair.......................	11
–	105	1074	Stuc Bheag	11
–	106	1072	Stob Coire Sgreamhach	3
63	107	1070	Braigh Coire Chruinn-bhalgain:........	6
–	108	1070	Puist Coire Ardair.................	9
64	109	1069	An Socach	12
65	110	1069	Meall Corranaich	2
66	111	1068	Sgurr Fhuaran	11
67	112	1068	Glas Maol.......................	7
–	113	1068	Creag a' Ghlas-uillt................	7
–	114	1068	Stob Coire an Lochain	1
–	115	1068	Stob Coire Dheirg	3
68	116	1064	Cairn of Claise....................	7
69	117	1062	An Teallach—Bidein a' Ghlas Thuill	14
–	118	1061	Beinn a' Ghlo—Airgiod Bheinn	6
70	119	1059	An Teallach—Sgurr Fiona	14
–	120	1059	Binnein Mor—South Top............	4
–	121	1056	Craig Coire nan Each	11
71	122	1055	Na Gruagaichean...................	4
72	123	1054	Liathach—Spidean a' Choire Leith......	13
73	124	1054	Toll Creagach	11
74	125	1053	Sgurr a' Chaorachain	12
75	126	1053	Stob Poite Coire Ardair	9
–	127	1053	Creag an Leth-choin (Lurcher's Crag) .	8
76	128	1052	Beinn a' Chaorainn..................	9
–	129	1052	Carn Ban Mor	8
77	130	1051	Glas Tulaichean....................	6
–	131	1051	Stob Poite Coire Ardair—East Top ...	9
–	132	1051	Eagle's Rock	7
–	133	1050	Beinn a' Chaorain—South Top.......	9
78	134	1049	Geal Charn.......................	4
79	135	1049	Sgurr Fhuar-thuill...................	12
–	136	1047c	Lord Berkeley's Seat...............	14
80	137	1047	Carn an t-Sagairt Mor...............	7
81	138	1047	Chno Dearg	4
–	139	1047	Creag an Fhithich	2
82	140	1046	Ben Wyvis—Glas Leathad Mor.........	15
83	141	1046	Cruach Ardrain	1
–	142	1046	Bidean an Eoin Dearg...............	12
84	143	1045	Beinn Iutharn Mhor	6
–	144	1045	Beinn a' Chaorainn—North Top......	9
–	145	1044c	An Leth-chreag	11

Table II.   Arranged in Order of Altitude   53

No. in order of Alt. Mtn.	Top	Height	Name	Sect. in Table I
85	146	1044	Stob Coir' an Albannaich..............	3
–	147	1044	White Mounth—Carn an t-Sagairt Beag	7
86	148	1043	Meall nan Tarmachan.................	2
–	149	1043	Stuc Mor.........................	11
87	150	1042	Carn Mairg........................	2
88	151	1040	Sgurr na Ciche.....................	10
–	152	1040	An Riabhachan—West Top..........	12
89	153	1039	Meall Ghaordie	2
90	154	1039	Beinn Achaladair....................	2
91	155	1038	Sgurr a' Bhealaich Dheirg	11
92	156	1037	Carn a' Mhaim	8
–	157	1036	Na Gruagaichean—North West Top...	4
–	158	1036	Sgurr na Lapaich....................	11
93	159	1035	Gleouraich	10
94	160	1034	Carn Dearg........................	4
95	161	1032	Am Bodach	4
96	162	1032	Creag Mhor	2
97	163	1032	Beinn Fhada (Ben Attow).............	11
–	164	1030	Creag Ghorm a' Bhealaich...........	12
98	165	1029	Carn an Righ	6
99	166	1029	Carn Gorm........................	2
100	167	1029	Ben Oss...........................	1
–	168	1029	Tom a' Choinich Beag	11
101	169	1027	Sgurr a' Mhaoraich.................	10
102	170	1027	Sgurr na Ciste Duibhe...............	11
–	171	1027	Meall Coire Choille-Rais	9
–	172	1026	Meall Garbh.......................	2
103	173	1025	Ben Challum	2
104	174	1024	Sgor Dhearg—Beinn a' Bheithir	3
105	175	1023	Liathach—Mullach an Rathain	13
106	176	1022	Buachaille Etive Mor—Stob Dearg......	3
107	177	1021	Aonach Air Chrith	10
–	178	1021	West Meur Gorm Craig	8
–	179	1020c	Corrag Bhuidhe.....................	14
108	180	1020	Ladhar Bheinn.....................	10
–	181	1020	Carn Dearg—South West Top........	4
109	182	1019	Mullach Coire Mhic Fhearchair.........	14
110	183	1019	Bheinn Bheoil	4
111	184	1019	Mullach Clach a' Bhlair	8
112	185	1019	Carn an Tuirc......................	7
–	186	1017	A' Choinneach......................	8
–	187	1015	Beinn a' Chaorainn Bheag...........	8
–	188	1015	Sgurr na Fearstaig	12
–	189	1014c	Sgor Iutharn......................	4
113	190	1013	Garbh Chioch Mhor	10
–	191	1013	Stacan Dubha	8
114	192	1012	Cairn Bannoch......................	7
–	193	1012	Meall Liath (Glen Lyon).............	2
115	194	1011	Beinn Ime.........................	1
–	195	1011	Stob na Doire.....................	3

No. in order of Alt. Mtn.	Top	Height	Name	Sect. in Table I
116	196	1010	Sgurr an Doire Leathain................	10
117	197	1010	Beinn Eighe—Ruadh-Stac-Mor.........	13
118	198	1010	The Saddle	10
119	199	1010	Beinn Udlamain......................	5
–	200	1010	The Saddle—Trig Point	10
–	201	1009	Drochaid Glas	3
120	202	1008	Sgurr Eilde Mor......................	4
121	203	1008	Beinn Dearg.........................	6
–	204	1008	Stob Coire na Cralaig	11
122	205	1007	Maoile Lunndaidh....................	12
–	206	1007	Beinn na Socaich	4
123	207	1006	Carn Liath	9
124	208	1006	An Sgarsoch.........................	6
–	209	1006	Gleouraich—Craig Coire na Fiar Bhealaich	10
125	210	1005	Beinn Fhionnlaidh....................	11
126	211	1004	Sgurr an Lochain.....................	10
127	212	1004	The Devil's Point.....................	8
–	213	1004	Meall a' Bharr	2
128	214	1003	Sgurr Mor...........................	10
129	215	1003	Aonach Meadhoin.....................	11
130	216	1002	Beinn an Dothaidh	2
131	217	1002	Sail Chaorainn.......................	11
–	218	1002	Sgurr na Carnach	11
–	219	1002	Beinn Achaladair—South Top	2
132	220	1001	Beinn a' Bheithir—Sgorr Dhonuill	3
133	221	1001	Sgor an Iubhair	4
134	222	1001	Meall Greigh	2
–	223	1001	Carn na Coire Mheadhoin	11
–	224	1001	Sron a' Choire (Ghoire on map)	9
–	225	1000c	Sgurr Creag an Eich	14
–	226	1000c	Beinn nan Eachan	2
135	227	1000	Sgurr Breac	14
–	228	1000	Fafernie	7
–	229	1000	Drochaid an Tuill Easaich	11
136	230	999	Sgurr Choinnich	12
137	231	999	A' Chailleach........................	14
138	232	999	Stob Ban............................	4
–	233	999	Creag a' Chaorainn..................	11
139	234	998	Broad Cairn.........................	7
140	235	998	Ben More Assynt.....................	16
141	236	998	Stob Diamh	3
–	237	998	Meall Dubhag	8
142	238	997	Glas Bheinn Mhor....................	3
–	239	997	Ben Challum—South Top	2
143	240	996	Spidean Mialach	10
–	241	996	Stob a' Ghlais Choire	3
–	242	996	Carn nam Fiaclan	12
144	243	995	An Caisteal.........................	1
145	244	994	Carn an Fhidleir or Carn Ealar	6

Table II. Arranged in Order of Altitude   55

| No. in order of Alt. | | | | Sect. in |
Mtn.	Top	Height	Name	Table I
146	245	994	Sgor na h'Ulaidh	3
147	246	993	Sgurr Alasdair	17
148	247	993	Sgurr na Ruaidhe....................	12
–	248	993	An Cearcallach	9
–	249	993	Mullach Cadha Rainich	11
149	250	992	Carn nan Gobhar (Sgurr na Lapaich group)..............................	12
150	251	992	Carn nan Gobhar (North of Glen Strathfarrar)	12
–	252	991c	Stob Ghabhar—Aonach Eagach	3
–	253	991c	Sron a' Ghearrain	3
151	254	991	Sgairneach Mhor	5
–	255	991	Sron Coire a' Chriochairean	9
–	256	991	Craig of Gowal	7
–	257	990c	Sgurr nan Spainteach	11
152	258	989	Beinn Eunaich	3
153	259	989	Sgurr Ban...........................	14
–	260	988	Sgurr an Fhuarail	11
154	261	987	Conival.............................	16
155	262	987	Druim Shionnach	10
156	263	987	Gaor Bheinn or Gulvain	10
157	264	987	Creag Leagach.......................	7
158	265	986	Lurg Mhor	12
159	266	986	Inaccessible Pinnacle of Sgurr Dearg	17
–	267	986	Mam nan Carn......................	6
160	268	985	Beinn Alligin—Sgurr Mhor	13
161	269	985	Ben Vorlich (Loch Earn)	1
–	270	984	Sgurr Thearlaich	17
–	271	983c	Stob a' Coire Liath Mhor	13
–	272	983	Creag an Dubh-loch	7
–	273	983	Cairn of Gowal	7
–	274	983	Sgurr an Lochan Uaine..............	8
162	275	982	An Gearanach	4
163	276	982	Ciste Dhubh.........................	11
164	277	982	Mullach na Dheiragain	11
165	278	981	Stob Coire a' Chairn.................	4
166	279	981	Maol Chinn-dearg....................	10
167	280	981	Creag Mhor	2
–	281	981	Sail Mhor	13
–	282	981	Glas Mheall Mor	14
–	283	981	Mullach Coire Mhic Fhearchair— East Top	14
168	284	980	Beinn a' Chochuill...................	3
169	285	980	Slioch—Trig Point	14
170	286	980	Cona' Mheall.......................	15
–	287	980	Slioch—North Top	14
–	288	980	Meikle Pap.........................	7
–	289	980	Stob Garbh.........................	3
171	290	978	Beinn Dubhchraig....................	1
–	291	978	Cairn of Sgurr Dearg	17

No. in order of Alt. Mtn.	Top	Height	Name	Sect.in Table I
172	292	977	Meall nan Ceapraichean...............	15
173	293	977	Stob Ban...........................	4
–	294	977	Meall Bhuidhe.....................	2
–	295	977	Meall Garbh.......................	4
174	296	976	Stob Coire Sgriodain..................	4
–	297	976	Meall Buidhe	8
–	298	975c	A' Choinneach Mhor	13
175	299	975	Beinn-a'-Ghlo—Carn Liath...........	6
176	300	975	Stuc a' Chroin	1
177	301	975	Carn a' Gheoidh	6
178	302	975	A' Mharconaich	5
–	303	975	An Garbhanach....................	4
179	304	974	Ben Lomond	1
180	305	974	Ben Sgritheall......................	10
–	306	974	Meall nam Peithirean	14
–	307	974	Sron nam Giubhas..................	3
–	308	974	Meall Mor	12
–	309	974	Meall Coire na Saobhaidhe	7
181	310	973	Sgurr a' Ghreadaidh	17
–	311	973	Little Glas Maol....................	7
–	312	973	Mullach Sithidh....................	11
–	313	972	Creag an Dail Mhor	8
–	314	972	Spidean Coire nan Clach	13
–	315	971	Sgurr Ban........................	13
–	316	970c	Stob a' Choire Mhail................	4
–	317	969	Sgurr a' Ghreadaidh—South Top.....	17
–	318	969	Meall an-t-Snaim...................	9
–	319	968c	The Saddle—West Top..............	10
–	320	968	Garbh Chioch Bheag................	10
–	321	968	Carn na Con Dhu	11
–	322	968	Stob an Fhuarain...................	3
182	323	967	Aonach Eagach—Sgor nam Fiannaidh...	3
–	324	967	Ceann Garbh	15
183	325	966	Ben More—Mull	17
–	326	966	Sgurr Choinnich Beag...............	4
–	327	966	Sron an Isean	3
–	328	966	Meall na Dige......................	1
184	329	965	Sgurr na Banachdich—North Peak......	17
185	330	965	Sgurr nan Gillean	17
–	331	965	Sgurr a' Bhuic	4
–	332	964	Bynack Beg	8
186	333	963	Meall Garbh.......................	2
187	334	963	Carn a' Chlamain	6
188	335	963	Sgurr Thuilm	10
–	336	963	Sgurr an Fhir Duibhe	13
–	337	963	Sgurr a' Dubh Doire	11
189	338	961	Ben Klibreck ......'...............	16
–	339	961	Gaor Bheinn—South Top	10
–	340	961	Druim Mor........................	7
–	341	961	Carn na Criche....................	14

Table II. *Arranged in Order of Altitude* 57

No. in order of Alt.				Sect. in
Mtn.	Top	Height	Name	Table I
190	342	960c	A' Mhaighdean	14
191	343	960c	Sgorr Ruadh.........................	13
–	344	960c	Ben More Assynt—South Top........	16
–	345	960c	Sgurr na Forcan....................	10
–	346	960c	Stob a' Choire Odhair...............	10
192	347	960	Meall Glas	2
193	348	960	Stuchd an Lochain	2
–	349	960	Stob Coire Sgriodain—South Top	4
194	350	959	Saileag	11
195	351	959	Beinn Fhionnlaidh....................	3
–	352	959	Cruach Ardrain—Stob Garbh........	1
196	353	958	Buachaille Etive Beag—Stob Dubh......	3
197	354	958	Bruach na Frithe	17
198	355	958	Tolmount...........................	7
–	356	958	Stob nan Clach	2
–	357	958	The Saddle—East Top	10
199	358	957	Tom Buidhe.........................	7
200	359	957	Carn Ghluasaid	11
201	360	957	Beinn nan Aighenan	3
202	361	956	Sgurr nan Coireachan.................	10
–	362	956	Meall an Fhuarain Mhoir	11
–	363	956	Sgurr Eilde Beag	4
203	364	955	Sgor Gaibhre	4
–	365	955	Tom a' Choinnich	15
–	366	955	Stob na Broige	3
–	367	955	Sron Coire na h'Iolaire..............	4
204	368	954	Beinn Liath Mhor Fannaich...........	14
205	369	954	Beinn Mhanach	2
206	370	954	Am Faochagach......................	15
–	371	954	Sail Liath	14
–	372	953c	Liathach—Northern Pinnacles	13
207	373	953	Sgurr nan Coireachan (Glen Dessary)....	10
208	374	953	Meall Dearg	3
–	375	953	Beinn Iutharn Bheag.................	6
–	376	952	Toll Creagach—West Top	11
–	377	952	Beinn Fhada........................	3
–	378	952	Carn a' Chlamain—North Top	6
209	379	951	Meal Chuaich........................	5
–	380	950c	Glas Mheall Liath	14
–	381	950c	Stob Cadha Gobhlach................	14
–	382	950	An Cabar	15
210	383	949	Meall Gorm	14
211	384	948	Sgurr Mhic Coinnich..................	17
212	385	948	Beinn Bhuidhe.......................	1
–	386	948	Sgurr a' Mhaoraich..................	10
–	387	948	A' Chioch..........................	11
213	388	947	Driesh	7
214	389	947	Creag a' Mhaim......................	10
–	390	947	Sgurr Sgumain	17
–	391	947	Sgorr Bhan.........................	3

No. in order of Alt. Mtn.	Top	Height	Name	Sect. in Table I
215	392	946	Meall Buidhe	10
216	393	946	Beinn a' Chroin	1
217	394	946	Carn Bhac	6
218	395	946	Beinn Tulaichean.	1
–	396	946	Creag Dhubh	12
219	397	945	Bidein a' Choire Sheasgaich.	12
220	398	945	Carn Dearg.	9
221	399	945	Sgurr na Sgine	10
222	400	944	An Socach—West Summit	6
223	401	944	Sgurr Dubh Mor	17
–	402	944	Sgurr na Sgine—North West Top	10
224	403	943	Stob a' Choire Odhair.	3
225	404	943	Ben Vorlich (Loch Lomond)	1
–	405	943	Am Bodach	3
–	406	943	Creag Leacach—South West Top	7
–	407	942	Carn Ban	9
–	408	942	Sgurr na Banachdich—Central Top . . .	17
–	409	942	Carn Cloich-mhuilinn.	8
226	410	941	Carn Dearg.	4
227	411	941	Carn na Caim.	5
228	412	940	Binnein Beag	4
–	413	940	Stob Coire nan Dearcag	11
–	414	940	Stob Coire Leith	3
–	415	940	Spidean Dhomhuill	10
229	416	939	Mount Keen	7
230	417	939	Luinne Bheinn	10
231	418	939	Mullach nan Coirean	4
–	419	939	Stob a' Bruaich Leith	3
–	420	939	Stob Coire Altruim	3
–	421	938	An Socach	6
–	422	938	Sgurr Dubh na Da Bheinn	17
–	423	938	Beinn a' Chroin—West Top.	1
–	424	937c	Corrag Bhuidhe Buttress	14
–	425	937c	Toman Coinich	14
232	426	937	Beinn na Lap	4
233	427	937	Beinn Sgulaird	3
–	428	937	Luinne Bheinn—East Top	10
–	429	937	Beinn Cheathaich	2
234	430	936	A' Bhuidheanach Bheag	5
235	431	935	Am Basteir	17
236	432	935	Sron a' Choire Ghairbh	10
237	433	935	Sgiath Chuil	2
–	434	935	East Meur Gorm Craig	8
238	435	934	Meall a' Chrasgaidh	14
239	436	933	Fionn Bheinn	14
240	437	933	Maol Chean-dearg.	13
241	438	933	The Cairnwell	6
242	439	933	Beinn Chabhair	1
–	440	933	Sgurr an Tuill Bhain	14
243	441	931	Beinn Bhreac	8

Table II.   Arranged in Order of Altitude   59

No. in order of Alt.				
Mtn.	Top	Height	Name	Sect. in Table I
244	442	931	Meall Buidhe—South East Top.........	2
245	443	931	Ben Chonzie (Ben-y-Chone)............	1
–	444	931	Ben Vorlich (Loch Lomond)— North Top	1
–	445	931	Beinn Fhada—North East Top	3
246	446	930c	Beinn Tarsuinn	14
–	447	930c	Stob Coire Gaibhre..................	4
–	448	930c	Sgurr a' Fionn Choire...............	17
247	449	930	A' Chailleach.......................	9
–	450	930	Meall Cruidh	3
–	451	930	Meall Buidhe	10
–	452	929	Tigh Mor na Seilge	11
–	453	929	Sgurr nan Saighead	11
–	454	929	Sgor Choinnich	4
248	455	928	Mayar.............................	7
249	456	928	Eididh nan Clach Geala	15
250	457	928	Meall nan Eun	3
251	458	928	Bla Bheinn (Blaven)	17
252	459	928	Moruisg	12
–	460	928	Ben Sgritheall—North West Top......	10
–	461	928	Glas Leathad Beag	15
–	462	928	Glas Mheall Mor	5
253	463	927	Ben Hope...........................	16
254	464	927	Seana Braigh	15
–	465	927	Am Fasarinen	13
–	466	927	Beinn Bhreac—West Top............	8
–	467	927	Sgurr Thormaid....................	17
255	468	926†	Ben Narnain........................	1
256	469	926	Geal Charn.........................	9
257	470	926	Meall a' Choire Leith	2
258	471	925	Beinn Liath Mhor	13
–	472	925	Stob Coire Raineach	3
259	473	924	Sgurr nan Eag	17
260	474	924	Creag Pitridh	4
–	475	924	Beinn a' Chuirn.....................	2
–	476	924	Bla Bheinn—South West Top	17
–	477	924	An Sgor (Glen Lyon)................	2
261	478	923	An Coileachan.......................	14
262	479	923	Sgurr nan Each	14
–	480	922c	Meall Ghlas Choire..................	4
–	481	922	Diollaid a' Chairn	4
–	482	922	Meall Odhar........................	7
–	483	922	Meall Gorm—South East Top........	14
–	484	922	Tom na Gruagaich	13
–	485	921	Mullach Coire nan Nead.............	4
–	486	920c	Carn Dearg—South East Top	9
263	487	920	Carn Sgulain	9
264	488	920	An Socach	11
–	489	920	Carn Bhac—South West Top.........	6
–	490	920	Geal Charn.........................	8

No. in order of Alt. Mtn.	Top	Height	Name	Sect. in Table I
–	491	920	Carn Balloch	9
–	492	920	Crow Craigies	7
265	493	919	Gairich	10
–	494	919	Sgurr Leac nan Each................	10
266	495	918	Sgurr a' Mhadaidh—South West Peak...	17
267	496	918	Ruadh Stac Mor	14
268	497	918	Creag nam Damh	10
269	498	918	A' Ghlas-bheinn	11
–	499	918	Tom na Sroine......................	4
–	500	918	Meall a' Churain	2
–	501	918	Mullach Coire Mhic Fhearchair-Sgurr Dubh...........................	14
–	502	918	Sron Chona Choirein	2
–	503	918	Tom Dubh	8
–	504	918	Meall Cunail	3
270	505	917	Carn Aosda	6
271	506	917	Meall na Teanga	10
272	507	917	Geal Charn.........................	5
–	508	917	Carn Bhinnein	6
–	509	917	Stob Coire Lochan	11
–	510	917	Mullach nan Coirean—South East Top	4
273	511	916	Beinn a' Chleibh	1
–	512	916	Creag na Caillich....................	2
–	513	916	Stob Coire Dhuibh	9
274	514	915	Ben Vane	1
275	515	915	Sgurr nan Ceannaichean..............	12
–	516	914c	Bhasteir Tooth.....................	17
276	517	914	Beinn a' Chlaidheimh................	14

† *927 on 1:10,000 map.*

INDEX TO TABLE I, MUNRO'S TABLES

Names in brackets indicate the locality, or the "separate mtn." to which the top belongs.
To facilitate reference in long sections, ¼, ½, ¾, has been added to the Section number to
indicate roughly the whereabouts of the name. Thus 7¼ means from about a quarter to
nearly half way through the Section; 7½, half to nearly three quarters through; and 7¾
from nearly three quarters to the end.

Name	Sect.	Name	Sect.
Coire na h-Iolaire, Sron	4	Doire, Stob na (Bu. Etive Mor) ...	3
Coire na Saobhaidhe, Meall......	7	Doire Leathain, Sgurr an	10
Coire nam Beith, Stob	3	Dorain, Beinn	2
Coire nan Dearcag, Stob	11	Dothaidh, Beinn	2
Coire nan Each, Craig	11	Driesh	7
Coire nan Lochan, Stob	3	Drochaid an Tuill Easaich	11
Coire nan Nead, Mullach	4	Drochaid Glas (Cruachan)	3
Coire Raineach, Stob	3	Druim Mor (Cairn of Claise)	7
Coire Sgreamhach, Stob.........	3	Druim Shionnach	10
Coire Sgriodain, Stob	4	Dubhag, Meall.................	8
Cona-mheall (Ross-shire)........	15	Dubhchraig, Beinn	1
Conbhairean, Sgurr nan........	11	Dubh, Creag (Carn nan Gobhar)..	12
Con Dhu, Carn na..............	11	Dubh Doire, Sgurr a'	11
Conival (Assynt)	16	Dubh-Loch, Creag an..........	7
Corrag Bhuidhe and Buttress.....	14	Dubh Mor, and Da Bheinn, Sgurr.	17
Corranaich, Meall..............	2	Dubh, Stob (Bu. Etive Bheag)	3
Craig of Gowal (Cairn Bannoch)..	7	Dubh, Sgurr (Mullach Coire	
Creag, see next word		Mhic F.)	14
Creagan a' Choire Etchachan	8¾		
Creag an Eich, Sgurr............	14	Each, Sgurr nan (Fannaich)......	14
Creise	3	Eachan, Beinn nan (Tarmachan)..	2
Criche, Carn na (Braeriach)......	8	Eag, Sgurr nan................	17
Criche, Carn na (Fannaich)	14	Eagle's Rock, Top of	7
Crow Craigies (Tolmount)	7	Ealar, Carn	6
Cruach Ardrain	1	Eas, Carn (Ben Avon)..........	8
Cruachan, Ben.................	3	East Meur Gorm Craig..........	8
Cruidh, Meall	3	Eibhinn, Beinn.................	4
Cuanail, Meall (Cruachan).......	3	Eich, Sgurr Creag an...........	14
Cuidhe Crom (Lochnagar).......	7	Eididh nan Clach Geala	15
Cul Choire, Stob an	4	Eige, Carn	11
		Eighe, Beinn..................	13
Dail Mhor, Creag an (Ben Avon) .	8	Eilde Mor and Eilde Beag, Sgurr..	4
Damh, Creag nan	10	Eun, Meall nan	3
Dearg, Beinn (Atholl)..........	6	Eunaich, Beinn	3
Dearg, Beinn (Ross-shire).......	15		
Dearg, Carn (Ben Nevis;		Fafernie (Cairn Bannoch).......	7
NW and SW)	4	Faochagach, Am...............	15
Dearg, Carn (Monadh Liadth)....	9	Fasarinen, Am (Liathach)	13
Dearg, Carn (Alder Dist.)........	4	Fearstaig, Sgurr na	12
Dearg, Carn (Loch Ossian)	4	Fhada, Beinn (Ben Attow)	11
Dearg Meadhonach, Carn	4	Fhada, Beinn (Glencoe)	3
Dearg, Meall (Glencoe)..........	3	Fhidleir, Carn an..............	6
Dearg, Sgurr (Cuillins)	17	Fhionnlaidh, Beinn (Ross)	11
Dearg, Stob (Cruachan)	3	Fhionnlaidh, Beinn (Argyll)......	3¾
Dearg, Stob (Bu, Etive Mor)	3	Fhir Duibhe, Sgurr an (Eighe)	13
Derry Cairngorm...............	8	Fhithich, Creag an (Lawers)......	2½
Devil's Point, The	8	Fhuarail, Sgurr an.............	11
Dhearg Sgorr (Beinn a' Bheithir)..	3	Fhuarain Mhoir, Meall an	11
Dhonuill Sgor	3	Fhuarain, Stob an	3¾
Diamh, Stob (Cruachan)	3	Fhuaran, Sgurr (Five Sisters)	11
Dige, Meall na (Stob Binnein)	1	Fhuar-thuill, Sgurr	12
Diollaid a' Chairn	4	Fiaclan, Carn nam.............	12

MUNROISTS

Here follows the list of those who have reported that they have completed (I) Munros, (II) Tops, (III) 3000 foot mountains in the British Isles furth of Scotland, Munros and Tops being those listed in the 1974 or earlier editions of the Tables. Future claims must be based on the 1981 Edition. Existing Munroists who are fit and well will be expected to do the new Munros and Tops as soon as possible as the accomplishment of this objective presents no insuperable task.

* denotes a member or former member of the S.M.C.

		Munros (I)	Tops (II)	Furth (III)
1.	*Rev. A. E. Robertson	1901	—	—
2.	*Rev. A. R. G. Burn	1923	1923	—
3.	*J. A. Parker	1927	—	1929
4.	*J. R. Corbett	1930	1930	—
5.	*J. Dow	1933	1947	1956
6.	J. Robertson	1938	—	—
7.	*G. G. Elliot	1938	—	—
8.	*A. L. Cram	1939	1939	—
	and	1978	1978	—
9.	J. Hirst	1947	1947	—
10.	Mrs Hirst	1947	1947	—
11.	*E. W. Hodge	1947	—	—
12.	*B. Horsburgh	1947	—	—
13.	*W. M. Docherty	1948	1948	1949
14.	W. D. McKinlay	1948	—	—
15.	J. Campbell	1949	—	—
16.	*C. V. Dodgson	1951	1951	—
17.	H. Hampton	1952	—	—
18.	*G. S. Ritchie	1953	—	—
19.	J. S. Anderson	1953	1953	1958
20.	*G. G. MacPhee	1954	1955	—
21.	*P. J. L. Heron	1954	—	1956
22.	*J. F. Hamilton	1954	—	1956
23.	*M. Hutchinson	1955	1955	—
24.	E. I. Lawson	1955	1955	—
25.	W. T. Allan	1956	—	—
26.	*J. Mallinson	1956	—	—
27.	*J. Ferrier	1956	—	—
28.	*G. Peat	1957	1967	—
29.	*J. A. Watt	1957	1957	1958
30.	E. Maxwell	1957	1957	1958
	and	1966	1966	—
31.	C. G. Macdonald	1958	—	—
32.	*J. Y. Macdonald	1958	—	—
33.	A. McKenzie	1958	—	1969
34.	J. C. Grant	1959	—	1961
35.	T. P. Kemp	1959	—	—
36.	Mrs J. Ferrier	1960	—	—

		Munros (I)	Tops (II)	Furth (III)
37.	Mrs M. J. Linklater-Shirras.........	1960	—	—
38.	Miss A. J. Littlejohn..............	1960	1960	1960
39.	Miss A. D. Miller..................	1960	—	1961
40.	*T. Nicholson	1960	1961	—
41.	Mrs K. M. Watson	1960	—	—
42.	J. R. Watson	1960	—	—
43.	*J. C. Donaldson	1961	—	—
44.	P. A. Larder......................	1961	—	1961
45.	P. N. L. Tranter	1961	—	—
	and	1964	—	—
46.	*J. C. I. Wedderburn	1962	—	—
47.	J. M. Burnett.....................	1962	—	—
48.	A. E. Robinson	1962	—	—
49.	K. D. Shaw.......................	1962	—	—
50.	Miss L. Ticehurst.................	1962	1962	1962
51.	*K. M. Andrew	1962	1969	—
52.	*G. H. Smith	1962	—	—
53.	*G. M. Smith......................	1963	1966	1968
	and	1969	1969	1971
54.	*W. L. Wood......................	1963	—	—
55.	J. A. Robertson...................	1963	—	—
56.	J. Cosgrove	1963	—	—
57.	*J. N. Ledingham	1963	—	—
58.	A. Farguharson...................	1963	—	—
59.	*A. R. Thrippleton	1964	—	—
60.	J. G. Fleming.....................	1964	—	—
61.	W. D. Fraser	1964	—	—
62.	*H. M. Brown	1965	1965	1967
	and	1969	—	1969
	and	1970	—	1971
	and	1974	—	—
	and	1975	—	—
63.	*W. T. Taylor	1965	1966	1967
64.	R. M. Milne	1965	—	—
65.	H. S. K. Stapley..................	1965	—	1965
66.	R. Hutchison	1965	—	—
67.	G. C. Sime	1966	1966	1969
68.	W. D. Nicholl	1966	—	—
69.	*D. C. H. Green	1966	1966	1969
70.	*G. King.........................	1966	—	—
71.	*D. Barclay	1966	—	—
72.	D. Hawksworth....................	1967	—	1969
73.	A. M. Fraser	1967	1980	1977
	and	1980	—	—
74.	A. C. Gardner	1967	—	1970
75.	Miss M. McCallum	1967	1968	—
76.	M. J. Moulton....................	1968	—	—
	and	1971	—	—
	and	1978	—	—
77.	R. Smith.........................	1968	1968	—
78.	Miss L. W. Urquhart	1968	—	—

		Munros (I)	Tops (II)	Furth (III)
79.	Mrs E. MacKay	1968	—	—
80.	A. J. Main	1968	—	—
81.	*R. D. Walton	1968	—	—
82.	W. Shand	1968	1968	1974
83.	G. G. Shand	1968	1968	1974
84.	R. L. Pearce	1968	—	—
85.	Barbara M. Tulloch	1968	—	—
86.	Helen M. Scrimgeour	1968	—	—
87.	*J. Hinde	1968	—	—
88.	R. W. G. Wood	1969	—	—
89.	I. T. Stephen	1969	—	—
90.	R. J. Grant	1969	—	—
91.	*W. T. Tauber	1969	—	—
92.	R. Hainsworth	1969	1969	—
93.	K. R. Cox	1969	1969	—
94.	R. Armour	1969	—	—
95.	Mrs E. R. Innes	1969	—	—
96.	W. G. Carter	1969	1970	1971
97.	B. Finlayson	1970	—	—
98.	J. W. Brydie	1970	—	—
99.	M. G. Geddes	1970	1970	—
100.	R. Gilbert	1971	—	—
101.	G. Downs	1971	—	—
102.	P. Edwards	1971	1980	1980
103.	I. Rae	1971	—	—
104.	I. Butterfield	1971	—	—
105.	J. Gillies	1971	—	—
106.	Andrew Nisbet	1972	—	—
107.	B. K. E. Edridge	1972	—	—
108.	*G. S. Roger	1972	—	—
109.	Colin Turner	1973	1973	—
110.	R. Cook	1973	1973	1973
111.	P. Roberts	1973	1975	—
112.	W. G. Barbour	1973	—	—
113.	D. Smith	1973	—	—
114.	K. MacLean	1973	—	—
115.	A. Robertson	1973	—	—
116.	J. Dawson	1973	—	—
117.	Ms D. Stadring	1973	—	—
118.	Janet Clark	1973	—	—
119.	John Mills	1973	—	—
120.	Don Smithies	1973	—	—
121.	W. C. T. Sarson	1973	1973	—
122.	A. L. Mackenzie	1973	—	—
123.	Archibald G. H. Grant	1973	—	—
124.	A. MacKenzie	1973	—	—
125.	A. R. Dunn	1974	—	—
126.	A. E. Lawson	1974	1974	1976
127.	D. J. Farrant	1974	—	—
128.	R. Hardie	1974	—	—
129.	J. W. Simpson	1974	—	—

		Munros (I)	Tops (II)	Furth (III)
130.	J. Sloane	1974	—	—
131.	L. MacKenzie	1975	—	—
132.	R. Millar	1975	—	—
133.	K. R. Cox	1976	—	—
134.	C. Marsden	1976	—	—
135.	D. Hunter	1976	—	—
136.	R. L. St. C. Murray	1976	1980	1980
137.	I. C. Spence	1976	—	—
138.	R. Payne	1976	—	—
139.	W. Douglas	1976	—	—
140.	M. Keates	1976	—	—
141.	E. Pilling	1976	—	—
142.	R. Morgan	1976	1976	1977
143.	A. E. Law	1976	—	—
144.	D. Tooke	1976	—	—
145.	R. Graham	1976	—	—
146.	*Campbell R. Steven	1976	—	—
147.	R. Davie	1976	—	—
148.	D. Whalley	1976	—	—
149.	T. MacDonald	1976	—	—
150.	D. Henderson	1976	—	—
151.	Murdo E. Macdonald	1977	—	—
152.	Erland Flett	1977	—	—
153.	A. N. Darbyshire	1977	—	—
154.	Jock Murray	1977	—	—
155.	Edward F. Emley	1977	—	1980
156.	R. D. Leitch	1977	—	—
157.	*W. Myles	1977	—	—
158.	M. H. MacKinnon	1977	—	—
159.	Denise Marsden	1977	1977	—
160.	W. M. Donaldson	1977	—	—
161.	A. F. des Moulins	1977	—	—
162.	Duncan C. Gray	1978	—	—
163.	Iain G. Gray	1978	—	—
164.	N. Hawkins	1978	—	—
165.	J. L. Morning	1978	—	—
166.	T. Moore	1978	—	—
167.	J. Allan	1978	—	—
168.	S. Robertson	1978	—	—
169.	A. S. Bowie	1978	—	—
170.	J. E. Smith	1978	—	—
171.	F. Wiley	1978	—	—
172.	I. C. Murray	1978	—	—
173.	I. C. Munro	1978	1978	—
174.	Mrs J. H. B. Bell	1978	1978	—
175.	A. G. MacLean	1978	—	—
176.	S. Craven	1978	—	—
177.	A. F. Craven	1978	—	—
178.	D. A. Shanks	1978	—	—
179.	R. C. Munro	1978	1978	—
180.	J. Stewart	1978	—	—

		Munros (I)	Tops (II)	Furth (III)
181.	Mrs A. L. Cram....................	1978	1978	—
182.	W. Steele	1978	—	—
183.	A. Stevens	1978	—	—
184.	S. Beck	1978	—	—
185.	Susan Mackenzie..................	1978	—	—
186.	C. E. Barton.....................	1979	—	—
187.	Ms. S. Robertson.................	1979	—	—
188.	D. A. Peet	1979	—	—
189.	David Lane.......................	1979	—	—
190.	A. L. Bartlet.....................	1979	—	1979
191.	P. Coper.........................	1979	1979	1976
192.	Carole Smithies...................	1979	—	—
193.	Pamela Brown....................	1979	—	—
194.	P. D. Brown......................	1979	—	—
195.	Leonard Jameson	1979	—	—
196.	M. R. Don	1979	—	—
197.	John Rogers......................	1979	—	—
198.	S. R. Palmer.....................	1979	—	—
199.	Dewi Jones.......................	1979	—	—
200.	F. Telfer	1979	—	—
201.	Mrs M. Tildesley	1979	—	—
202.	H. Thomson......................	1979	—	—
203.	D. Foster	1979	—	—
204.	Christopher Bond	1980	—	—
205.	Tom Rix	1980	—	—
206.	I. H. Chuter	1980	—	—
207.	Ivan Waller	1980	—	—
208.	Mr Brian David and			
209.	Mrs Patricia Batty.................	1980	—	—
210.	† Archie Mitchell	1973	—	—
211.	Fergus McIntosh..................	1979	1980	1980
212.	W. Ross Napier	1980	—	—
213.	Ronald Leask.....................	1980	1980	—
214.	Sue Jardine.......................	1980	—	—
215.	D. Alistair Baird	1980	—	—
216.	Jeremy Fenton....................	1980	—	—

† *entry received too late for insertion in current order.*

ERRATUM
MUNROISTS
Names of Munroists added after printing but before publication of the 1981 edition of the Tables

			Munros (I)	Tops (II)	Furth (III)
217.		J. R. M. Lubbock	1976	-	-
218.		F. D. Binnie	1977	-	-
219.	*	R. Hillcoat	1980	-	-
220.		Peter Edward	1980	-	-
221.		Raymond Hutcheson	1980	-	-
222.		Ronald Crawford	1980	-	-
223.		Carole M. Davie	1980	-	-
224.		Stanley Grant	1980	-	-
225.		Alan L. Brook	1980	1980	1978
226.		M. W. McCue	1980	1980	1980
227.	*	Donald Mill	1980	-	-
228.		Alan Gately	1980	-	-
229.		Stan Bradshaw	1980	1980	1980
230.		John Howarth	1980	1980	1980
231.		C. R. Knowles	1980	1980	-
232.	*	Trevor Ransley	1980	-	-
233.		Sheila Cormack	1980	-	-
234.		Anne McGeachie and	1980	-	-
235.		George McGeachie	1980	-	-
236.		R. W. J. Webster	1981	-	-
-		Matthew Moulton and	1980	-	-
-		H. M. Brown and	1979	-	1978
		and	-	1979

ERRATUM
Amendments to the list of Munroists

33. Should be A. G. McKenzie and should show "and 1980" under (I) and (III)
55. Change to I. A. Robertson.
58. Alter to Farquharson.
191. The surname should be Cooper.
160. Change to W. A. Donaldson.

Add asterisks to the following who are S.M.C. members.

99. M. G. Geddes.
106. Andrew Nisbet.
129. J. W. Simpson.
171. Fred Wylie.

Corrections require to be made as follows.
MUNROS
Pages 16 and 60. Meall Cunail should be Meall Cuanail.
Page 37. Beinn Fhionnlaidh and page 39 An Socach. Bart sheet number 54.
CORBETTS
Sec. 2. The Bart sheet number for Beinn an Lochain and the rest of the section should be 48. Height of Meall an Fhudair is 764 and that of Stob a' Choin 865.
Sec. 5. Sgurr Inse and Cruach Inse. In both these cases Inse should be Innse.
Sec. 10. Garbh Bheinn. The height should be 885.
Sec. 11. Beinn Fhionnlaidh and Sec. 12. An Socath. The Bart sheet number is 54.

(page to be inserted after page 72.)

Corbett's Tables

SCOTTISH MOUNTAINS 2500 FEET
AND UNDER 3000 FEET IN HEIGHT
WITH RE-ASCENT OF 500 FEET ON ALL SIDES

by J. ROOKE CORBETT

Edited and revised by J. C. Donaldson and Hamish M. Brown

FOREWORD

J. ROOKE CORBETT did not publish his List of 2500-feet mountains, all of which he himself had ascended, probably because he felt that before doing so some further checking on the ground would be desirable. After his death it was passed by his sister to the Guide Books General Editor, who decided that it was worthy of record as of interest and assistance to hill walkers generally, and it was printed as he left it subject to some minor amendments.

There was no indication in Corbett's papers as to the criterion he adopted in listing the heights included, but it seems clear that his only test was a re-ascent of 500 feet on all sides to every point admitted, no account being taken of distance or difficulty. A detailed check of the latest maps has been made for this Edition resulting in 17 peaks being added to the List while 11 have been removed from it. The Section numbering has been revised, listing first areas south of the Great Glen, then those to the north followed by the Islands. In each Section the hills are placed in a mainly south to north order. 762m is taken as the equivalent of 2500 feet but, as O.S. figures are to the nearest metre only, a hill given a height of 762m on an O.S. map cannot be accepted as a Corbett without checking that the exact height is not below 762m.

The List remains not strictly comparable with those compiled by either Munro or Donald as it does not profess to include all "summits" and "tops" from 2500 to 2999 feet, which on a Munro or Donald basis would give a much larger total.

Changes made to the 1974 Edition

Number listed in the 1974 Edition of the Tables   217

Removed from List in this Edition:

Old Section No.	5b	Beinn Chumhain. Does not have a re-ascent of 500 feet on all sides.

Old Section No. 5b Beinn Chumhain. Does not have a re-ascent of 500 feet on all sides.

6 Carn Easgann Bana. Does not have a re-ascent of 500 feet on all sides.

Carn na Laraiche Maoile. Height now exceeded by that of Carn na Saobhaide, formerly of equal status.

7a Druim Garbh. Does not have a re-ascent of 500 feet on all sides.

7b Druim Fiaclach. Replaced by Sgurr na Ba Glaise.

7c Beinn an Tuim. Does not have a re-ascent of 500 feet on all sides.

Meall Coire nan Saobhaidh. Replaced by Meall na h-Eilde.

7d Bhuidhe Bheinn. Replaced by Sgurr a' Bhac Chaolais.

9 Sgurr nan Ceannaichean. Promoted to Munro status.

15 Sgor Mor. Does not have a re-ascent of 500 feet on all sides.

Meall Uaine. Does not have a re-ascent of 500 feet on all sides.

Total removed   11
_____
206

Added to List in this Edition:

New Section No. 2 Beinn an Lochain. Reduced from Munro.

3 Cam Chreag.

5 Meall Ligiche.

6 Sow of Atholl.

Meall na Meoig of Ben Pharlagain.

9 Corrieyairack Hill. Equal height with Gairbeinn.

10 Beinn na Uamha.

Sgurr na Ba Glaise. In place of Druim Fiaclach.

Beinn Mhic Cedidh.

11 Sgurr Cos na Braechd-Laoidh.

Sgurr a' Bhac Chaolais. In place of Bhuidhe Bheinn.

12 Meall na h-Eilde. In place of Meall Coire nan Saobhaidh.

14 Sgurr Gaorsaic.

15 Beinn Liath Mhor a' Ghiubhais Li.

Little Wyvis.

16 Sail Gorm, Quinag.

18 Beinn Talaidh, Mull.

Total added   17
_____

Total number of Corbetts in this Edition   223

SCOTTISH MOUNTAINS OF 2500 FEET
AND UNDER 3000 FEET IN HEIGHT
WITH RE-ASCENT OF 500 FEET ON ALL SIDES

		Map Sht. Nos.		Map
Name	*Height*	*O.S.*	*Bart.*	*Reference*

SECTION 1

South of the Forth-Clyde Canal

Shallow on Minnoch..............	768	77	37/40	405907
Kirriereoch Hill	786	77	37/40	420871
Merrick..........................	843	77	37	428855
Corserine	814	77	37/40	497871
Cairnsmore of Carsphairn	797	77	40	594980
Hart Fell........................	808	78	40/41	114136
White Comb......................	822	79	41	163151
Broad Law	840	72	41	146235
Cramalt Craig	830	72	41	169247

SECTION 2

Loch Fyne to Balquhidder and Loch Earn

Beinn Bheula	779	56	44	151983
Ben Donich	847	56	48	218043
The Brack.......................	787	56	48	246031
Ben Arthur (The Cobbler)	884	56	48	259058
Beinn Luibhean	858	56	—	243079
Beinn an Lochain	901	56	44	218079
Binnein an Fhidleir	817*	56/50	44	230109
Meall an Fhudair.................	746	56	44	271192
Beinn a' Choin...................	770	56/50	44	354130
Stob a' Choin....................	845	56	44	416161
Ceann na Baintighearna**..........	771	57	44	474163
Ben Vane	821	57	44	535137
Ben Ledi........................	879	57	44	562098
Meall na Fearna..................	809	57	44	651186

*The highest point is 1500m east of the name on the map.
**Highest point lies 1400m south of name on map.

Name	Height	Map Sht. Nos. O.S.	Map Sht. Nos. Bart.	Map Reference

SECTION 3

Loch Etive, Glen Orchy and Auch

Name	Height	O.S.	Bart.	Map Reference
Beinn a' Bhuiridh	897	50	47	094283
Beinn Chuirn	880	50	48	281292
Beinn Mhic-Mhonaidh	793	50	48/47	209350
Beinn Udlaidh	840	50	48	280333
Beinn Bhreac-Liath	803	50	48	304339
Beinn Odhar.....................	900	50	48	338338
Beinn Chaorach..................	818	50	48	359328
Cam Chreag.....................	885†	50	48	375346
Beinn a' Chaisteal	883	50	48	348364
Beinn nam Fuaran................	802	50	48	361382
Creach Bheinn...................	810	50	47	024422
Beinn Trilleachan	840	50	47	086439
Stob Dubh, Beinn Ceitlin	883	50	47/48	166488

†*Height from 1:25,000 O.S. There is, therefore, a re-ascent of 500 feet on all sides.*

SECTION 4

Glen Lyon, Breadalbane and Glenalmond

Name	Height	O.S.	Bart.	Map Reference
Beinn nan Imirean................	844	51	48	419309
Meall an t-Seallaidh	852	51	48	542234
Creag MacRanaich	809	51	48	546256
Creag Uchdag	879	51	48	708323
Creagan na Beinne	887	51	48	744369
Meall Luaidhe	780	51	48	586436
Beinn nan Oighreag...............	909	51	48	543414
Meall nan Subh	804	51	48	461397
Meall Buidhe	901	51	48	426449
Cam Chreag.....................	862	51	48	536491
Beinn Dearg.....................	830	51	48	609497
Meall nan Tairneachan............	787	52	48	807544
Auchnafree Hill..................	789	52	48	809309
Farragon Hill....................	783	52	48	804553

SECTION 5

Appin and Etive to Glen Spean

Name	Height	O.S.	Bart.	Map Reference
Fraochaidh.....................	879	41	47	029517
Meall Ligiche...................	772	41	47	094528
Beinn Maol Chaluim..............	847	41	47	135526
Beinn Mhic Chasgaig	862	41	47	221502
Beinn a' Chrulaiste	857	41	50/48	246567
Garbh Bheinn	867	41	50/51	169601

Name	Height	Map Sht. Nos. O.S.	Bart.	Map Reference

SECTION 5 *(continued)*

Name	Height	O.S.	Bart.	Map Reference
Mam na Gualainn	796	41	50	115625
Glas Bheinn	789	41	50	259641
Leum Uilleim.....................	906	41	51	331641
Sgurr Inse.......................	808	41	51	290748
Cruach Inse	857	41	—	280763

SECTION 6

Loch Rannoch to Loch Laggan and Badenoch

Name	Height	O.S.	Bart.	Map Reference
Meall na Meoig of Ben Pharlagain ...	865	42	51	448642
Stob an Aonaich Mhoir	855	42	51	537694
Beinn Mholach	841	42	51/48	587655
Beinn a' Chuallaich................	892	42	51/48	684618
Meall na Leitrach	775	42	51	639703
Sow of Atholl....................	803	42	51	624741
The Fara.........................	911	42	51	598844
An Dun...........................	827	42	51	716802
Craig an Loch	867	42	51	735807
Meallach Mhor	769	35	51	777909
Carn Dearg Mor	857	35	51	824912

SECTION 7

Atholl, Glen Feshie, Glen Shee and Deeside

Name	Height	O.S.	Bart.	Map Reference
Ben Vrackie	841	43	51	951632
Ben Vuirich	903	43	51/52	997700
Ben Gulabin.....................	806	43	51/52	101722
Monamenach.....................	807	43	52	176707
Beinn Mheadonach................	901	43	—	880758
Beinn Bhreac	912	43	51	868821
Leathad an Taobhain	912	43	51	822858
Sgor Mor (Glen Dee)..............	813	43	51	006914
Creag nan Gabhar.................	834	43	51/52	154841
Morrone.........................	859	43	51/52	132886
Conachcraig.....................	865	44	52	280865
Ben Tirran	896	44	52	373746
Mount Battock	778	44	52	550844
Carn na Drochaide	818	36/43	52	127938
Creag an Dail Bheag*	862	36/43	52	158981
Culardoch	900	36/43	52	193988
Brown Cow Hill..................	829	36	52	221044
Morven..........................	871	37	52	377040

Carn Liath at MR 165977 is also 862m and is more prominent from Braemar.

Name	Height	Map Sht. Nos. O.S.	Bart.	Map Reference

SECTION 8

Avon, Don and Rinnes

Name	Height	O.S.	Bart.	Map Reference
Creag Mhor	895	36	52	057048
Meall a' Buachaille	810	36	52	991115
Geal Charn	821	36	52	090127
Carn Ealasaid	792	36	52	228118
Carn Mor	804	37	52	265183
Cook's Cairn	774*	37	56	299275
Corryhabbie Hill	781	37	56	281289
Ben Rinnes†	840	28	56	255355

*400m south-east from the point where the name appears on the map.
†On the 1:10,000 map the highest point of Ben Rinnes is named Scurran of Lochterlandoch. This name is also given on Bartholomew's map.

SECTION 9

Glen Roy, Corrieyairack and the Monadh Liath

Name	Height	O.S.	Bart.	Map Reference
Beinn Iaruinn	800c	34	50	296900
Carn Dearg (south of Glen Roy)	834	34	51	345887
Beinn Teallach	913	34	51	361859
Carn Dearg (north of Glen Roy)	768	34	51	357948
Carn Dearg (Gleann Eachach)	815	34	51	349967
Gairbeinn	896	34	51	460985
Corrieyairack Hill	896	34	51	429998
Carn Chuilinn	816	34	51	416034
Meall na h'Aisre	862	35	51	515000
Carn na Saobhaidhe	811	35	51	600145
Carn an Fhreiceadain	878	35	51	726071
Geal-charn Mor	824	35	51	837124

c denotes a contour

SECTION 10

Loch Linnhe to Lochailort and Glenfinnan

Name	Height	O.S.	Bart.	Map Reference
Fuar Bheinn	766	49	47	853564
Creach Bheinn	853	49	50	871577
Garbh Bheinn	805	40	50	904622
Beinn Resipol	845	40	50	766655
Beinn na h-Uamha	762†	40	50	918665
Sgurr Dhomhnuill	888	40	50	889679
Carn na Nathrach	786	40	50	887699
Rois-Bheinn	882	40	50	756778
Sgurr na Ba Glaise	874	40	50	770777
An Stac	814	40	50	763793

Name	Height	Map Sht. Nos. O.S.	Bart.	Map Reference
SECTION 10 *(continued)*				
Beinn Mhic Cedidh	783	40	50	829788
Beinn Odhar Bheag...............	882	40	50	846778
Druim Tarsuinn..................	770	40	50	875727
Sgurr Ghiubhsachain	849	40	50	876751
Sgorr Craobh a' Chaorainn	775	40	50	895758
Sgurr an Utha	796	40	50	885839
Streap..........................	909	40	50	946863
Braigh nan Uamhachan	765	40	50	975867
Stob Coire a' Chearcaill	770	41	—	017727
Meall a' Phubuill.................	774	41	50	029854

†*Most precise height available from O.S. who state that if it had been plotted originally in imperial units it would have been published as 2500 ft.*

SECTION 11

Loch Morar to Glen Shiel

Name	Height	Map Sht. Nos. O.S.	Bart.	Map Reference
Carn Mor	829	33	50	903910
Sgurr na h'Aide..................	867	33	50	889931
Sgurr Cos na Breachd-laoidh*.......	835	33	50	948947
Fraoch Bheinn...................	858	33	50	986940
Sgurr Mhurlagain	879	33	50	012944
Sgurr an Fhuarain................	901	33	50	987980
Ben Aden	887	33	50	899986
Beinn Bhuidhe...................	855	33	50	822967
Sgurr Coire Choinnichean	796	33	50	791011
Beinn na Caillich	785	33	50	796067
Sgurr a' Choire-bheithe	913	33	50	895015
Sgurr nan Eugalt	894	33	50	931045
Sgurr a' Bhac Chaolais............	885	33	50	958110
Beinn na h'Eaglaise...............	804	33	50	854120
Beinn nan Caorach	773	33	50	871122
Sgurr Mhic Bharraich.............	778	33	50	917174
Am Bathach.....................	798	33	50	073144

*Possibly an O.S. misprint for laoigh.

SECTION 12

Loch Lochy, Loch Cluanie and Gleann Fhada

Name	Height	Map Sht. Nos. O.S.	Bart.	Map Reference
Beinn Bhan......................	771	34	50	141857
Geal Charn......................	804	34	50	156943
Meall na h-Eilde	838	34	50	185946
Ben Tee.........................	901	34	50	241972
Meall Dubh	788	34	50	245078
Druim nan Cnamh	789	34	50	131077
Carn a' Choire Ghairbh	863	34	50	137189
Aonach Shasuinn	889	34	50	173180

Name	Height	Map Sht. Nos. O.S.	Map Sht. Nos. Bart.	Map Reference

SECTION 13

Applecross and Torridon

Name	Height	O.S.	Bart.	Map Reference
Sgurr a' Chaorachain†	792	24	54	797417
Bheinn Bhan	896	24	54	804450
Beinn Damh	902	24	54	893502
Beinn Dearg	914*	24	54	895608

*Exact height is 2998 ft.
†Spelt Ghaorachain in 1:50,000 map.

SECTION 14

Loch Duich, Strathcarron and Glen Strathfarrar

Name	Height	O.S.	Bart.	Map Reference
Sgurr Gaorsaic	838	25	54	036219
Sgurr an Airgid	841	25	54	940227
Sgumain Coinntich	879	25	54	977304
Faochaig	868	25	54	022317
Aonach Buidhe	899	25	54	058324
Sgorr na Diollaid	818	25	55	282362
Beinn Dronaig	797	25	54	037382
Beinn Tharsuinn	863	25	54	055433
Sgurr na Feartaig	862	25	55	055454
An Ruadh-stac	892	25	55	922481
Fuar Tholl	907	25	55	975489
Sgorr an Lochan Uaine	873	25	55	969531
Sgurr Dubh	782	25	54	979558
An Sidhean	814	25	55	171454
Bac an Eich	849	25	55	222489
Meallan nan Uan	840	25	—	264545
Sgurr a' Mhuilinn	879	25	55	265558
Beinn a' Bha'ach Ard	862	26	55	361435

SECTION 15

Loch Maree, Braemore, Freevater and Diebidale to Wyvis

Name	Height	O.S.	Bart.	Map Reference
Baosbhein	800	19/24	54	871654
Beinn an Eoin	855	19	54	905646
Ruadh-stac Beag	896	19	54	973614
Meall a' Ghiubhais	878	19	54	978638
Beinn Airigh Charr	791	19	58	930762
Beinn Lair	860	19	58	982732
Creag Rainich	807	19	58	097751
Beinn a' Chaisgein Mor	857	19	58	983785
Beinn Dearg Mor	908	19	58	032799
Beinn Dearg Bheag	818	19	58	020811

Name	Height	Map Sht. Nos. O.S.	Bart.	Map Reference
SECTION 15 *(continued)*				
Sail Mhor	767	19	58	033887
Beinn Liath Mhor a' Ghiubhais Li ...	766	20	59	281713
Beinn Enaiglair	889	20	58	225805
Beinn a' Chaisteil	787	20	59	370801
Carn Ban	845	20	58	339876
Carn Chuinneag	838	20	59	484833
Little Wyvis	764	20	59	430645

SECTION 16

Coigach, Assynt and Loch Merkland

Name	Height	O.S.	Bart.	Map Reference
Cul Beag.........................	769	15	58	140088
Cul Mor	849	15	58	162119
Canisp...........................	846	15	58	203187
Creag Liath	814	15	58	287158
Glas Bheinn	776	15	58	255265
Spidean Coinich, Quinag	764	15	58	205278
Sail Gharbh, Quinag...............	808	15	58	209292
Sail Gorm, Quinag	776	15	58	198304
Beinn Leoid	792	15	58	320295
Meallan Liath Coire Mhic Dhughaill .	801	15	58	357392
Ben Hee	873	16	60	426339

SECTION 17

The Far North

Name	Height	O.S.	Bart.	Map Reference
Arkle............................	787	9	58	303462
Meall Horn.......................	777	9	58	353449
Ganu Mor, Foinaven	908	9	58	317507
Cranstackie	800	9	58	351556
Beinn Spionnaidh	772	9	58	362573
Beinn Loyal	764	10	60	578489

SECTION 18

The Islands

Name	Height	O.S.	Bart.	Map Reference
HARRIS				
Clisham	799	13	57	155073
SKYE				
Glamaig	775	32	54	514300
Garbh-bheinn	806	32	54	531232
RHUM				
Askival.......................	812	39	50	393952
Ainshval......................	781	39	50	379944

Name	Height	Map Sht. Nos. O.S.	Bart.	Map Reference
MULL				
Beinn Talaidh	762†	49	47	625347
Dun da Ghaoithe................	766	49	47	672362
JURA				
Paps of Jura—..................				
Beinn an Oir....................	784	61	43	498749
ARRAN				
Goat Fell.......................	874	69	44	991415
Beinn Tarsuinn	825	69	44	959412
Cir Mhor	798	69	44	973432
Caisteal Abhail	859	69	44	969444

†*Beinn Talaidh. Highest point lies 25m south west of the pillar and is 2502 ft.*

Donald's Tables

ALL HILLS IN THE SCOTTISH LOWLANDS
2000 FEET IN HEIGHT AND ABOVE

by PERCY DONALD, B.Sc.

Revised by J. C. Donaldson and Hamish M. Brown

INTRODUCTION

Mr Percy Donald visited every elevation of 2000 feet and over at least once before issuing his Tables and he discarded many of the points examined as unworthy of inclusion as "Tops". His method of determining "Hills" and "Tops" is described in the Explanation of Tables.

The editors' revision is based on the latest O.S. 1:50,000 maps available but where they do not provide essential information reference has been made to larger scale maps. Scrutiny of these maps has yielded two additional tops, one in Section 5, the other in Section 12, and 12 points have been added to the appendix.

The total number of "Hills" is 86 and of "Tops" 135. The most northerly hill is Innerdownie in the Ochils, the most easterly† Cairn Hill (not named on any map) on The Cheviot, if tops are considered, otherwise Windy Gyle in the Cheviots. The most southerly is Cairnsmore of Fleet, and the most westerly Shallow on Minnoch, both in Galloway (extreme points in the last two cases are actually tops, Knee of Cairnsmore and Shallow on Minnoch, North Top).

†*Cauldcleuch Head in Roxburgh is the most easterly hill wholly in Scotland.*

EXPLANATION OF TABLES

Table 1

In this Table the following natural grouping has been adopted:—

Section	Area	Hills	Tops
1	Ochil Hills	5	9
2	Moorfoot Hills	5	5
3	Tinto...	1	1
4	Enclosed by the Biggar-Broughton-Moffat roads	5	8
5	Enclosed by the Broughton-Innerleithen-St Mary's Loch-Tweedsmuir roads.................................	13	21
6	Enclosed by the Tweedsmuir-St Mary's Loch-Moffat roads	10	21
7	Enclosed by the Moffat-St Mary's Loch-Tushielaw-Eskdalemuir roads	9	15
8	Between the Abington-Moffat and New Cumnock-Thornhill roads	12	15
9	Between the New Cumnock-Thornhill and Dalmellington-New Galloway roads...............................	6	10
10	Between the Dalmellington-New Galloway Station and Girvan-Creetown roads	18	26
11	Cauldcleuch Head...................................	1	1
12	Cheviot Hills (on Union Boundary)	1	3
		86	135

Section 12 includes also five hills wholly in England.

An Appendix gives particulars of 28 additional elevations not meriting inclusion as tops, but all enclosed by an isolated 610m (2000-feet) contour. These have been included in order that the Table may be a complete record of every separate area of ground reaching 610m (2000-feet) in accordance with Mr Donald's policy.

Column 1. Name. The Ordnance Survey spelling is always followed, an * implying that the name appears only on the 1:10,000 or 6-inch maps. Where no name appears on any map the top has been given the name of its hill with North, South, etc., Top added. The number in this column is merely for convenience of reference from Tables II and III.

Column 2. Height. Heights are the latest available from the Ordnance Survey and it should be borne in mind that there have been many changes since publication of the 1:50,000 1st series. 610m have been taken as the equivalent of 2000 feet.

Columns 3 and 4. Hill and top numbers. These give the number in order of altitude of such tops as may be considered separate hills and their subsidiary tops respectively.

"Tops" and "Hills" were determined by Mr Donald in accordance with the following rules:—

"Tops". All elevations with a drop of 100 feet (30.48m) on all sides and elevations of sufficient topographical merit with a drop of between 100 feet and 50 feet (15.24m) on all sides.

"Hills". Grouping of "tops" into "hills", except where inapplicable on topographical grounds, is on the basis that "tops" are not more than 17 units from the main top of the "hill" to which they belong, where a unit is either $\frac{1}{2}$ mile measured along the connecting ridge or one 50-feet contour between the lower "top" and its connecting col.

While the rules as they stand rather lack mathematical precision, the actual result of their application is that, with but few exceptions, an 80-feet (24.38m) drop determines a "top" and the 17-unit rule a "hill".

Columns 5 and 6. Maps. Sheet numbers have been given for the O.S. 1:50,000 and Bartholomew's 1:100,000 maps. It should be borne in mind that there are variations in spellings between the two publications and that heights do not always agree while a number of names are omitted from the latter map.

Column 7. Six figure map references have been used the use of which is explained on all 1:50,000 maps.

The columns giving summit and fences details have been omitted as a great deal of the information is out of date.

Table II

This Table gives the Scottish "hills" and "tops" only (including the three on the Union Boundary), arranged in order of height.

Columns 1 and 2 give the hill and top numbers, as given in columns 3 and 4 of Table I.

Column 3 gives the height. c denotes a contour.

Column 4 gives the name, as given in column 1 of Table I.

Column 5 gives a reference to the Section number and the number of the top in that section so as to enable it to be readily found in Table I.

Table III

This is an alphabetical index to Table I and contains the name of every "hill", "top", and other elevation listed therein.

TABLE I

Name	Height	Hill No.	Top No.	Map Sht. No. O.S.	Map Sht. No. Bart.	Map Reference
SECTION 1—OCHIL HILLS						
1. Blairdenon Hill	631	71	109	58	45	866018
2. Ben Ever......................	622	—	121	58	45	893001
3. Ben Cleuch....................	721	25	37	58	45	903006
4. The Law......................	638	—	104	58	45	910996
5. Andrew Gannel Hill*	670	—	73	58	45	919006
6. King's Seat Hill	643	66	94	58	45	936998
7. Tarmangie Hill	645	64	91	58	45	942014
8. Whitewisp Hill.................	643	—	98	58	45	955014
9. Innerdownie..................	611	83	130	58	45	966031
SECTION 2—MOORFOOT HILLS						
1. Windlestraw Law	659	58	82	73	41	372431
2. Whitehope Law................	621	79	122	73	41	330446
3. Bowbeat Hill	625	75	117	73	41	292469
4. Blackhope Scar	651	62	89	73	41	315483
5. Jeffries Corse or Dundreich......	622	78	120	73	41	275491
SECTION 3—TINTO HILLS						
Tinto.......................	707	28	44	72	40	953344
SECTION 4—CULTER HILLS						
1. Coomb Dod...................	635	—	107	72	40	046238
2. Hillshaw Head................	653	61	88	72	40	048246
3. Gathersnow Hill†.............	690	41	58	72	40	059257
4. Coomb Hill	639	—	102	72	40	069264
5. Hudderstone**	627	73	114	72	40	022272
6. Culter Fell	748	13	18	72	40	053291
7. Chapelgill Hill	696	33	49	72	40	068304
8. Cardon Hill	676	—	68	72	40	065315

†*Also named as Glenwhappen Rig on many maps.*
***Formerly named Heatherstone Law.*

SECTION 5—MANOR HILLS						
1. Talla Cleuch Head* (Muckle Side)	690	39	56	72	41	134218
2. Clockmore	640	—	100	72	41	183229
3. Broad Law	840	2	2	72	41	146235
4. Cramalt Craig	830	3	3	72	41	169248
5. Greenside Law................	643	67	95	72	41	198256
6. Hunt Law....................	639	—	103	72	41	150265
7. Fifescar Knowe	808	—	8	72	41	176269
8. Dollar Law...................	817	5	5	72	41	178278

Name	Height	Hill No.	Top No.	Map Sht. No. O.S.	Map Sht. No. Bart.	Map Reference

SECTION 5 *(continued)*

Name	Height	Hill No.	Top No.	O.S.	Bart.	Map Reference
9. Taberon Law	637	—	105	72	41	146289
10. Middle Hill..............	732	20	28	72	41	159294
11. Drumelzier Law.............	668	51	74	72	41	149313
12. Pykestone Hill..................	737	18	24	72	41	173313
13. The Scrape	716	—	41	72	41	176324
14. Deer Law	629	—	111	73	41	223256
15. Black Law	696	34	50	73	41	218275
16. Black Law—North East Top†....	696	—	51	73	41	224280
17. Blackhouse Heights.............	675	—	71	73	41	222290
18. Dun Rig	743	16	22	73	41	253316
19. Glenrath Heights..............	726	22	31	73	41	241323
20. Stob Law	676	47	67	73	41	230333
21. Birkscairn Hill..................	661	56	80	73	41	275332

†*Southern end of Blackhouse Heights on 6" map but not named.*

SECTION 6—MOFFAT HILLS

Name	Height	Hill No.	Top No.	O.S.	Bart.	Map Reference
1. Nether Comb Craig (Top above)..	723	—	35	78	—	129110
2. Swatte Fell	728	21	29	78	41	118114
3. Falcon Craig* (Top above).......	723	—	34	78	—	123127
4. Saddle Yoke..................	735	—	26	78	41	144124
5. Under Saddle Yoke*............	732c	15	21	78	—	143126
6. Hart Fell......................	808	7	7	78	41	114136
7. Whitehope Heights*............	625c	74	116	78	—	095139
8. Cape Law	721	24	36	78	41	131151
9. Din Law	665	—	77	78	41	124157
10. Great Hill......................	774	—	15	78	—	145165
11. Garelot Dod....................	690	40	57	78	41	125173
12. Erie Hill	689	42	59	78	41	124188
13. Carlavin Hill	727	—	30	78	41	140190
14. Laird's Cleuch Rig* (Top above)..	682	—	62	72	—	125197
15. Carrifran Gans	748	—	19	79	41	158137
16. White Comb....................	822	4	4	79	41	163151
17. Firthhope Rig..................	801	—	10	79	41	153154
18. Lochcraig Head.................	800	8	11	79	41	167176
19. Molls Cleuch Dod	784	10	13	79	41	152180
20. Nickies Knowe..................	760	—	17	79	—	164192
21. Garelet Hill	680	—	64	72	—	124201

SECTION 7—ETTRICK HILLS

Name	Height	Hill No.	Top No.	O.S.	Bart.	Map Reference
1. Loch Fell	688	43	60	79	41	170047
2. West Knowe*..................	655c	—	87	79	—	164053
3. Wind Fell	664	54	78	79	41	179062
4. Hopetoun Craig.................	632	—	108	79	—	188068
5. Ettrick Pen.....................	692	36	53	79	41	199077
6. Croft Head.....................	636	70	106	79	41	153057
7. Capel Fell	678	45	65	79	41	164069
8. Smidhope Hill*	643	—	97	79	—	168077

Name	Height	Hill No.	Top No.	Map Sht. No. O.S.	Map Sht. No. Bart.	Map Reference

SECTION 7 *(continued)*

Name	Height	Hill No.	Top No.	O.S.	Bart.	Map Reference
9. White Shank	620	—	124	79	41	169082
10. Bodesbeck Law	662	55	79	79	41	169103
11. Bell Craig	624	76	118	79	41	187129
12. Andrewhinney Hill	677	46	66	79	41	198139
13. Mid Rig	644	—	93	79	41	206144
14. Trowgrain Middle	627	—	115	79	41	208149
15. Herman Law	614	82	127	79	41	214157

SECTION 8—LOWTHER HILLS

Name	Height	Hill No.	Top No.	O.S.	Bart.	Map Reference
1. Queensberry	697	31	47	78	40	989998
2. Earncraig Hill	610	86	134	78	40	973013
3. Gana Hill	668	52	75	78	40	954011
4. Wedder Law	666	53	76	78	40	938025
5. Glenleith Fell	611	—	131	78	40	922023
6. Scaw'd Law	661	57	81	78	40	922034
7. Ballencleuch Law	691	38	55	78	40	935049
8. Rodger Law	688	—	61	71/78	40	945058
9. Comb Law	643	68	96	71/78	40	944075
10. Cold Moss	628	—	113	71/78	40	898094
11. East Mount Lowther	631	72	110	71/78	40	877100
12. Lowther Hill	725	23	33	71/78	40	890107
13. Green Lowther	732	19	27	71/78	40	901120
14. Dun Law	675	48	69	71/78	40	917136
15. Lousie Wood Law	618	81	126	71/78	40	932152

SECTION 9—CARSPHAIRN HILLS

Name	Height	Hill No.	Top No.	O.S.	Bart.	Map Reference
1. Beninner	710	—	43	77	40	606972
2. Cairnsmore of Carsphairn	797	9	12	77	40	595980
3. Moorbrock Hill	651	63	90	77	40	621984
4. Dugland	610c	—	135	77	40	602009
5. Windy Standard	698	30	46	77	40	620015
6. Alhang	640c	69	99	77	40	643011
7. Alwhat	629	—	112	77	40	647021
8. Meikledodd Hill	640	—	101	77	—	661028
9. Blacklorg Hill	680	44	63	77	40	654043
10. Blackcraig Hill	700	29	45	77	40	648065

SECTION 10—GALLOWAY HILLS

Name	Height	Hill No.	Top No.	O.S.	Bart.	Map Reference
1. Larg Hill	675	49	70	77	37	425757
2. Lamachan Hill	716	26	39	77	37	435770
3. Curleywee	674	50	72	77	37	454769
4. Millfore	656	60	85	77	37	478755
5. Benyellary	719	—	38	77	37	414838
6. Merrick	843	1	1	77	37	428855
7. Kirriereoch Hill	782	11	14	77	37/40	420871
8. Tarfessock—South Top	620	—	123	77	——	413886

Name	Height	Hill No.	Top No.	Map Sht. No. O.S.	Map Sht. No. Bart.	Map Reference

SECTION 10 *(continued)*

	Name	Height	Hill No.	Top No.	O.S.	Bart.	Map Reference
9.	Tarfessock	697	32	48	77	37/40	409892
10.	Shallow on Minnoch	768	12	16	77	37/40	405907
11.	Shallow on Minnoch—North Top.	659	—	84	77	—	400920
12.	Craignaw	645	65	92	77	37	459833
13.	Dungeon Hill	610c	85	133	77	37/40	461851
14.	Mullwharcher	692	37	54	77	37/40	454867
15.	Meikle Millyea	746	14	20	77	37	518829
16.	Milldown	738	17	23	77	37	510839
17.	Millfire	716	—	40	77	37	508848
18.	Corserine	814	6	6	77	37/40	498871
19.	Carlin's Cairn	807	—	9	77	37/40	496883
20.	Meaul	695	35	52	77	37/40	501910
21.	Cairnsgarroch	659	59	83	77	37/40	515914
22.	Bow.........................	613	—	128	77	37/40	508928
23.	Coran of Portmark	623	77	119	77	37/40	509937
24.	Knee of Cairnsmore	656	—	86	77	37	509654
25.	Cairnsmore of Fleet	711	27	42	77	37	502671
26.	Meikle Mulltaggart	612c	—	129	77	37	512678

SECTION 11—ROXBURGH HILLS

	Name	Height	Hill No.	Top No.	O.S.	Bart.	Map Reference
	Cauldcleuch Head	610c	84	132	79	41	458008

SECTION 12—CHEVIOT HILLS

SCOTLAND AND ENGLAND

	Name	Height	Hill No.	Top No.	O.S.	Bart.	Map Reference
1.	Windy Gyle	619	80	125	80	41	855152
2.	Auchope Cairn	726	—	32	80	41	891198
3.	Cairn Hill—West Top...........	737†	—	25	80	41	896193

ENGLAND

	Name	Height	Hill No.	Top No.	O.S.	Bart.	Map Reference
4.	The Cheviot	815	—	—	74	41	909205
5.	Hedgehope Hill	714	—	—	80	41	944197
6.	Comb Fell....................	650	—	—	80	41	919187
7.	Bloodybush Edge	610	—	—	80	41	902144
8.	Cushat Law	615	—	—	80	41	928137

†*The highest point on the Union Boundary. Not named on either O.S. or Bartholomew maps.*

SECTION 13—APPENDIX

The following points are not "tops", but each is enclosed by an isolated 610m (2000-ft.) contour. Donald listed 15 of these points to which have been added points 16-28 all taken from the O.S. 1:50,000 map. Bartholomew map sheet numbers have not been given for this section as few of the points are shown on these maps.

	Name	Height	O.S. Sht. No.	Map Reference
1.	Greenforet Hill*	616	58	862019
2.	Conscleuch Head.................	621	73	221263

Name	Height	O.S. Sht. No.	Map Reference

SECTION 13 *(continued)*

Name	Height	O.S. Sht. No.	Map Reference
3. White Cleuch Hill	611	73	229298
4. Birks Hill	619	73	282337
5. Jeffries Corse—North Top	611	73	281495
6. Shielhope Head or Water Head......	613	72	191253
7. Greenside Law—South Top.........	611	72	197252
8. Whitehope Knowe*.................	614	78	098144
9. Ellers Cleuch Rig.................	611	78	127167
10. Comb Head—East Top	610c	71	902092
11. Millfore—South Top	620	77	472751
12. Bow—South Top..................	612	77	505925
13. Bow—Middle Top.................	610c	77	507927
14. Keoch Rig*......................	610c	77	618000
15. Trostan Hill	610c	77	611017
16. Stake Law.......................	679	73	263321
17. Hundleshope Heights	685	73	250339
18. Windlestraw Law—S.W. Top†......	654	73	363421
19. Mathieside Cairn.................	664	72	130222
20. Lamb Knowe	661	72	167225
21. Tods Knowe......................	691	72	163232
22. Great Knock.....................	691	72	139256
23. Brown Knowe*	686c	72	142249
24. Notman Law	734	72	185260
25. Long Grain Knowe	703	72	167295
26. Peden Head*	686c	71	906124
27. Dungrain Law	667	71	911130
28. Firthybrig Head..................	763	79	158172

†*Not named on any map.*

TABLE II

THE 2000-FEET TOPS ARRANGED IN ORDER OF ALTITUDE

Hill No.	Top No.	Height	Name	Ref. to Table I
1	1	843	Merrick...............................	10-6
2	2	840	Broad Law	5-3
3	3	830	Cramalt Craig	5-4
4	4	822	White Comb...........................	6-16
5	5	817	Dollar Law............................	5-8
6	6	814	Corserine	10-18
7	7	808	Hart Fell..............................	6-6
—	8	808	Fifescar Knowe	5-7
—	9	807	Carlin's Cairn	10-19
—	10	801	Firthhope Rig..........................	6-17
8	11	800	Lochcraig Head........................	6-18
9	12	797	Cairnsmore of Carsphairn	9-2
10	13	784	Molls Cleuch Dod	6-19
11	14	782	Kirriereoch Hill	10-7
—	15	774	Great Hill.............................	6-10
12	16	768	Shallow on Minnoch...................	10-10
—	17	760	Nickies Knowe........................	6-20
13	18	748	Culter Fell	4-6
—	19	748	Carrifran Gans	6-15
14	20	746	Meikle Millyea........................	10-15
15	21	745	Under Saddle Yoke*...................	6-5
16	22	743	Dun Rig	5-18
17	23	738	Milldown	10-16
18	24	737	Pykestone Hill........................	5-12
—	25	737	Cairn Hill (West Top).................	12-3
—	26	735	Saddle Yoke..........................	6-4
19	27	732	Green Lowther........................	8-13
20	28	732c	Middle Hill...........................	5-10
21	29	728	Swatte Fell	6-2
—	30	727	Carlavin Hill	6-13
22	31	726	Glenrath Heights......................	5-19
—	32	726	Auchope Cairn	12-2
23	33	725	Lowther Hill..........................	8-12
–	34	723	Falcon Craig* (Top above)..............	6-3
–	35	723	Nether Coomb Craig (Top above)..........	6-1
24	36	721	Cape Law.............................	6-8
25	37	721	Ben Cleuch...........................	1-3
—	38	719	Benyellary	10-5
26	39	716	Lamachan Hill........................	10-2
—	40	716	Millfire..............................	10-17
–	41	716	The Scrape	5-13
27	42	711	Cairnsmore of Fleet	10-25
—	43	710	Beniner..............................	9-1
28	44	707	Tinto................................	3-—
29	45	700	Blackcraig Hill........................	9-10

Hill No.	Top No.	Height	Name	Ref. to Table 1
30	46	698	Windy Standard	9-5
31	47	697	Queensberry...........................	8-1
32	48	697	Tarfessock	10-9
33	49	696	Chapelgill Hill	4-7
34	50	696	Black Law	5-15
—	51	696	Black Law (North East Top)	5-16
35	52	695	Meaul	10-20
36	53	692	Ettrick Pen............................	7-5
37	54	692	Mullwharcher	10-14
38	55	691	Ballencleuch Law	8-7
39	56	690	Talla Cleuch Head......................	5-1
40	57	690	Garelot Dod...........................	6-11
41	58	690	Gathersnow Hill	4-3
42	59	689	Erie Hill	6-12
43	60	688	Loch Fell	7-1
—	61	688	Rodger Law	8-8
—	62	682	Laird's Cleuch Rig* (Top above)..........	6-14
44	63	680	Blacklorg	9-9
—	64	680	Garelet Hill	6-21
45	65	678	Capel Fell	7-7
46	66	677	Andrewhinney Hill	7-12
47	67	676	Stob Law	5-20
—	68	676	Cardon Hill	4-8
48	69	675	Dun Law..............................	8-14
49	70	675	Larg Hill.............................	10-1
—	71	675	Blackhouse Heights.....................	5-17
50	72	674	Curleywee............................	10-3
—	73	670	Andrew Gannel Hill*	1-5
51	74	668	Drumelzier Law........................	5-11
52	75	668	Gana Hill	8-3
53	76	666	Wedder Law...........................	8-4
—	77	665	Din Law	6-9
54	78	664	Wind Fell	7-3
55	79	662	Bodesbeck Law	7-10
56	80	661	Birkscairn Hill........................	5-21
57	81	661	Scaw'd Law	8-6
58	82	659	Windlestraw Law	2-1
59	83	659	Cairnsgarroch	10-21
—	84	659	Shallow on Minnoch (North Top)..........	10-11
60	85	656	Millfore	10-4
—	86	656	Knee of Cairnsmore	10-24
—	87	655c	West Knowe*...........................	7-2
61	88	653	Hillshaw Head.........................	4-2
62	89	651	Blackhope Scar	2-4
63	90	651	Moorbrock Hill........................	9-3
64	91	645	Tarmangie Hill	1-7
65	92	645	Craignaw	10-12
—	93	644	Mid Rig...............................	7-13
66	94	643	King's Seat Hill	1-6
67	95	643	Greenside Law.........................	5-5
68	96	643	Comb Law	8-9

Hill No.	Top No.	Height	Name	Ref. to Table 1
—	97	643	Smidhope Hill*	7-8
—	98	643	Whitewisp Hill.........................	1-8
69	99	640c	Alhang	9-6
—	100	640	Clockmore	5-2
—	101	640	Meikledodd Hill	9-8
—	102	639	Coomb Hill	4-4
—	103	639	Hunt Law.............................	5-6
—	104	638	The Law	1-4
—	105	637	Taberon Law	5-9
70	106	636	Croft Head............................	7-6
—	107	635	Coomb Dod	4-1
—	108	632	Hopetoun Craig........................	7-4
71	109	631	Blairdenon Hill	1-1
72	110	631	East Mount Lowther....................	8-11
—	111	629	Deer Law	5-14
—	112	629	Alwhat	9-7
—	113	628	Cold Moss	8-10
73	114	627	Hudderstone	4-5
—	115	627	Trowgrain Middle......................	7-14
74	116	625c	Whitehope Heights*	6-7
75	117	625	Bowbeat Hill	2-3
76	118	624	Bell Craig	7-11
77	119	623	Coran of Portmark	10-23
78	120	622	Jeffries Corse..........................	2-5
—	121	622	Ben Ever..............................	1-2
79	122	621	Whitehope Law........................	2-2
—	123	620	Tarfessock (South Top)	10-8
—	124	620	White Shank	7-9
80	125	619	Windy Gyle	12-1
81	126	618	Lousie Wood Law......................	8-15
82	127	614	Herman Law	7-15
—	128	613	Bow..................................	10-22
—	129	612c	Meikle Mulltaggart	10-26
83	130	611	Innerdownie...........................	1-9
—	131	611	Glenleith Fell	8-5
84	132	610c	Caldcleuch Head.......................	11-—
85	133	610c	Dungeon Hill	10-13
86	134	610	Earncraig Hill	8-2
—	135	610c	Dugland	9-4

TABLE III

ALPHABETICAL INDEX TO TABLE I

DISTRICT GUIDE BOOKS
TO SCOTLAND

Since the new series S.M.C. district guide books commenced publication in 1968 many requests have been received for an outline of the divisions in Scotland covered by the main series of eight volumes. *Munro's Tables* and the *Mountains of Scotland* are additional volumes in the series covering the whole of Scotland in their respective subjects. The map reproduced on the opposite page shows the eight divisions represented by the main series.

The Scottish Mountaineering Club Journal, published annually in July, is a useful source of additional information about mountaineering in the areas covered by these Tables. Every year it describes new routes and first ascents and reports significant changes in mountain shelters, bridges, paths and general access, as well as alterations to designated mountain heights and the status of Munros and Tops. Additions to the record of Munroists which appears on pages 68 to 72 are published in the S.M.C. Journal.

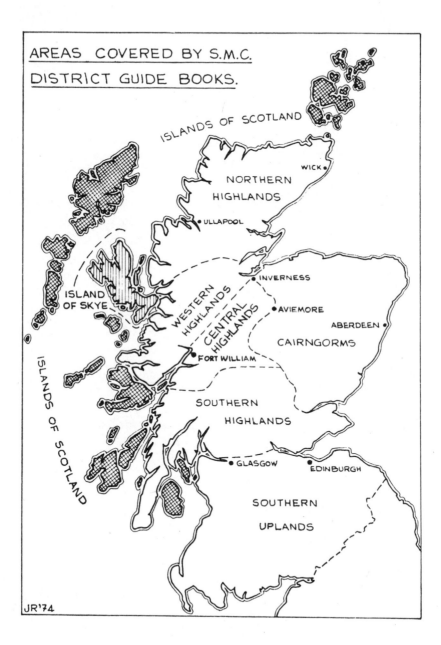

AREAS COVERED BY S.M.C.
DISTRICT GUIDE BOOKS.

ISLANDS OF SCOTLAND

NORTHERN HIGHLANDS

WICK

ULLAPOOL

INVERNESS

ISLAND OF SKYE

WESTERN HIGHLANDS

CENTRAL HIGHLANDS

AVIEMORE

ABERDEEN

CAIRNGORMS

FORT WILLIAM

ISLANDS OF SCOTLAND

SOUTHERN HIGHLANDS

GLASGOW

EDINBURGH

SOUTHERN UPLANDS

JR'74